PITA
THE GREAT

BY VIRGINIA T. HABEEB

Illustrations by Emanuel Schongut

WORKMAN PUBLISHING, NEW YORK

Library of Congress Cataloging-in-Publication Data
Habeeb, Virginia T. Pita The Great.
Includes index.   1. Pita bread.   2. Cookery, Near Eastern.   I. Title.
TX770.P56H33 1986   641.8′15   85-40902   ISBN 0-89480-039-6

Art Director: Susan Aronson Stirling
Book design: Carol Dietz
Cover and book illustrations: Emanuel Schongut

Workman Publishing
1 West 39 Street
New York, NY 10018

Manufactured in the United States of America
First printing June 1986

10 9 8 7 6 5 4 3 2 1

DEDICATION

This book is dedicated with love to
my mother Rose, my dearest inspiration,
and my father, Mitchel, who could accept
nothing less than perfection, especially
in mother's pita bread. It was!

ACKNOWLEDGMENTS

Working with these recipes and refining those handed down from family to family has been a labor of love. And living with *Pita the Great,* even more! It has filled me with many warm memories of family and friends and it has opened up a world of understanding in the gastronomic differences that abound from region to region in the Middle East.

I feel about work as did the venerable Kahlil Gibran, who was a friend of my father during their early years together in America, and who said, ''Work is love made visible. And if you cannot work with love, but only with distaste, it is better that you should leave your work and sit at the gate of the temple and take alms of those who work with joy.''

My warmest thanks to my family and friends who have offered their suggestions and recipes and especially to:

● Mitchell Habeeb, my husband, whose critical taste and discerning palate would refine even the most perfect recipe.

● Suzanne Rafer who first saw the potential of combining the age-old tradition of baking pita with the first health foods of civilization and who has been a constant source of inspiration.

● My editor, Susan Gough Henly who conceived of blending the culinary heritage of the Middle East with the eclectic foods of today and who has made the book work so beautifully.

● Bob Gilbert, who tested the recipes, making certain we had refined our directions for your ease of understanding and preparation.

CONTENTS

3

PITA ALONG-SIDES

4

PITA INSIDES

5

PITA
SWEETS

A Word From The Author

Although I grew up in the wonderful and majestic hills of West Virginia, both my parents were Middle Eastern and I was steeped in their heritage. In my earliest childhood days I was introduced to the versatility and tasty goodness of pita, it being the center of every family meal and party occasion.

Having always enjoyed the pleasures of pita—the same "miracle" loaves of Bible history that I learned about in Sunday school—I am not at all surprised that it has become the "in" bread of health-conscious America today.

In our home, my mother lovingly baked pita every week and delighted in serving it with all the delicious foods that showed it at its best—*hummus bi tahini, baba ghanouge,* and all sorts of delicious lamb concoctions such as *kibbeh,* stuffed grape leaves, and yogurt soup with pita dumplings, to name a few.

Later on, when I traveled throughout the Middle East I explored the streets or "souks" of old Jerusalem and Cairo with their stalls laden with lamb, fish, olives, squash, sesame seeds, legumes, tomatoes, nuts, figs, oranges, and lemons. I saw townspeople take their homemade pita dough to be baked in commercial ovens or *furh-ins* for the evening meal and watched delivery boys and old men carry mounds of baked pita to the streetside markets. And, I can still taste the sumptuous appetizers we sampled from elaborate *meze* trays in the courtyards of Caesaria.

Pita continues to play a central role in our everyday meals and when we entertain. My husband, Mitchell Habeeb, also of Middle-Eastern ancestry, makes all our own yogurt and yogurt cheese. He tells some exciting tales of his days as a U.S. Army officer in the Middle East. The most appealing to me are the stories of his early-morning breakfasts of pita, yogurt cheese, plump black olives, fresh cucumbers, and tomatoes, which have now become a staple for us.

In my professional career as a home economist and food editor I have been able to combine my love of pita and pita-based recipes with an eclectic knowledge of and fascination with all types of food. I hope you will share my passion as you enjoy *Pita the Great.*

Virginia T. Habeeb
June, 1986

PITA THE GREAT

In ancient times it was believed to be the staff of life; today it is newly acknowledged as the tastiest and most versatile natural food: pita, the puffed little loaf with the pocket in the middle, comes to us from the very cradle of our civilization.

Stories tell of bedouins wandering the desert plains under the sweltering sun. When night fell and the temperature dropped they would pitch their tents and prepare the evening meal. Mixing a batch of powdered grain and water, they'd pat it into flat rounds and "bake" it over an open fire, probably atop the same vessel used to mix the dough. The milk that the bedouins carried in their sheepskin and goatskin bags would also, by night, have become a thick and tangy custard-like curd: the first yogurt and a perfect pita accompaniment.

From its traditional beginnings as the mainstay of simple nomad fare and exotic

Middle Eastern feasts, pita has made an amazing conquest of the American palate. Not only is it associated with the traditional *Shish Kebab* and other sublime Middle-Eastern classics like *Hummus Bi Tahini*, *Baba Ghanouge*, *Falafel*, *Kefta Kebabs*, *Kibbeh*, and *Tabbouleh*. Now it scoops up Oriental Shrimp and Black Bean Dip, Basil Fondue Piedmontese, and Chicken Liver Pâté; is a pocketful of seafood, chicken, vegetable, fruit, and nut salads; is transformed into tarts, triangles, croutons, pyramids, crêpes, and pies; and can even be dropped into soups as dumplings.

Pita is known by many names depending upon its country or region of origin. And, also depending upon the recipe itself and the way it is handled or baked, it may or may not have a pocket in the middle. In Greece it is called *pita* and is usually pocketless, *pide* in Turkey, *kemaj* in Lebanon, *aysh* in Egypt, *khubiz* in Syria and Morocco, *kesra* in Algeria. In America we've adopted the Greek term *pita* even though our bread has a pocket.

Whatever its origin and name, pita is a lightly leavened round loaf (measuring anywhere from five to nine inches) with a soft crust and generally a hollow center. Usually made without shortening or milk, it is baked in a very hot oven for only a few minutes. It puffs quickly as it bakes but falls slightly when it is removed from the oven and cools. Hence, its famous pocket, the Pandora's box for creative cooks everywhere.

Some versions are made

Pita appeals to Americans because it is healthy, convenient, and versatile. You can split it, tear it or roll it, you can fill it, wrap it, dip it, top it; you can bake it, fry it, and toast it; you can make it and buy it.

Low in sodium, fat, and calories, pita is most often matched with yogurt, olives, cucumbers, tomatoes, bulgur, chickpeas, eggplant, sesame seeds, nuts, and the natural sweeteners: dates, apricots, oranges, pomegranates, and quince—foods born of the earliest civilizations. Given our current fascination with this chewy, flavorful bread, we are now enjoying the world's first health foods in new and creative combinations.

Let this book be your inspiration as it draws on the age-old culinary traditions of the Middle East and then takes off with a cornucopia of enticing new recipes that throw open all the marvelous possibilities that pita presents.

without any leavening and are baked on top of the range on a concave pan. The Lebanese *marook* is shaped by hand in much the same manner as pizza, by tossing and stretching the dough until it is well over a foot in size. It is then flipped onto a concave-shaped metal surface set over a heat source where it bakes quickly in minutes. The Armenians have a similar bread, called *lavash,* which is baked to a cracker-like crispness and measures anywhere from five to twenty inches.

ABOUT THE RECIPES

• Recipes throughout are interchangeable as pita gowiths. Many of the appetizers may be used for sandwiches. Salad and sandwich fillings may be served as appetizers. All may be extended into full-course meals with some creative imagination.

• Throughout *Pita The Great*, I've suggested a specific kind of pita for each recipe. You can, of course, substitute your favorite pita variation for what is listed. It is an accommodating bread for an uncommonly limitless variety of uses.

• All yields are approximate. Creative cooks may shrink or stretch ingredients at will as they adjust recipes to include more, less, or additional ingredients. I have indicated yields for salad sandwiches, dips, and spreads in cup measurements rather than number of servings. Depending on what other dishes you are offering and how large your pitas are, you can then decide how much you want to serve each person.

• Where appropriate, Middle Eastern names are given along with the English recipe titles. A brief explanation of the Middle Eastern name and origin is also included.

• With all Middle Eastern and Mediterranean recipes, seasonings and proportions for similar classic recipes will vary from region to region in the countries of their origin. Keep in mind that these recipes are general guidelines. I have given you fairly basic proportions for each recipe which you can adjust and experiment with according to your personal taste. This is best described as *"the-more-or-less-principle."* Take for example *Hummus Bi Tahini*, page 40. If you like a tart flavor, use *more* lemon juice. If you are a garlic devotee, use *twice* as much. This is creative cookery at its best. Be adventuresome!

• The abundant use of herbs and spices in the recipes enhances the flavor of pita. Such piquantly seasoned dishes lend themselves to the elimination or reduction of salt for a healthier diet.

• Most Middle Eastern meat recipes call for lamb, however its beef or veal counterpart is acceptable. Those who are on special diets may substitute ground turkey for ground lamb or beef with the exception of Bulgur and Lamb Tartare, page 53. In recipes where lamb only is mentioned, it is preferable.

• Butter is lightly salted unless otherwise noted. For clarified butter, see page 56.

• On broiling meat and seafood *kebabs* I've given you general guidelines on distances away from the heat but it is wise to follow the directions for the particular range you are using.

• A blender or food processor is a must. Many of the recipes call for chopped, minced, diced, mashed, or puréed ingredients and these appliances shortcut such tedious tasks.

PITA AND YOGURT

Contained in this chapter are my tried and true secrets to baking perfect pita every time. Before you start read the general tips and individual recipes carefully and you're sure to be rewarded with light, chewy pitas complete with drip-free pockets. And, once you've made your own pitas you'll be hooked forever and won't think twice about whipping up a batch of Herbed Zahter Pita to go with Herb-Broiled Chicken and Onion, or Griddle-Baked Pita (the easi-est of all) for Pita Cheese Crêpes with Orange-Blossom Syrup. In addition, I show you how to make pita toast, crou-tons, and crisps.

Also in this chapter are our family rec-ipes for yogurt, yo-gurt cheese, and white cheese—classic pita ac-companiments in the Middle-East and now popular as part of the American diet in this health-conscious age. While a yogurt-making appliance is handy, my recipe shows you how to make yogurt on your kitchen range with a mini-mum of fuss. All these prod-ucts are good sources of cal-cium, riboflavin, and protein and contain none of the fillers and preservatives that are so common in many commercial variations.

SECRETS TO BAKING PERFECT PITA

Rolling and Baking

• Handle the dough carefully. Reserve enough of a draft-free work surface to place as many rolled pitas as 24 small or 12 large.

• The key to rolling a smooth well-rounded pita loaf is to roll from the center of each ball of dough, giving the dough a ¼ turn after each roll. Carefully flip the circles over to smooth out any creases that might prevent a pocket from forming.

• As you roll out each ball, cover the remaining balls with towels that you have sprinkled very lightly with warm water to keep the surface of the dough supple and moist.

• It will take approximately 30 minutes to roll out 24 small pitas. By the time you have rolled the last pita begin baking the first ones you have rolled which have then risen for 30 minutes. Remember to preheat the oven and baking sheet 15 minutes before the pitas have finished rising.

• A very hot oven is a must. Make certain the oven has returned to temperature before baking each batch and don't keep opening the oven to check on the pitas while they are baking. The high heat makes the dough rise and puff literally in seconds. The bread bakes quickly, in minutes and browns lightly on the bottom. If you want a more golden top, flip small pitas over after 4 minutes, large ones after 3 to 3½ minutes and bake up to 1 minute longer; be careful not to let the loaves get crisp and brittle.

• Pita bakes and puffs best on a preheated baking sheet placed on the bottom rack of the oven. Bake 1 sheet at a time for best results. For pitas that don't puff (Herbed Zahter Pita and Sweetened-Sesame Pita) you may bake 2 sheets at once. Add a second rack in the oven close to the first rack. Place 1 sheet on each rack, staggering 1 on the right and 1 on the left, and reverse the sheets from the top to bottom racks halfway through baking for even heat distribution.

• Whatever you do remember practice makes perfect!

Cutting

• To make a single sandwich pocket, cut off the top of the pita leaving just enough space to gain access to the inside easily.

• To make 2 pocket sandwiches, cut a medium or large pita in half.

• To make 2 pancakes or rounds (for use as bases for tarts or wraps for fillings), slit a pita completely around.

• To make small wedges for appetizers, cut a medium pita into 6 triangles; to make larger wedges for sandwich snacks, cut a larger pita into 6 or 8 triangles.

Storage and Thawing

• Wrap baked pitas immediately as they come from the oven in clean, dry cotton dish towels (keep plenty on hand) until they are cool enough to handle. Then remove the warm pitas from the towels and place them in plastic bags. The insides of the bags will develop a slight moisture condensation as the loaves cool, which will keep them soft. Let the loaves cool completely before sealing the bags and storing.

• Store pita in plastic bags in the refrigerator for up to 1 week or in the freezer for up to 3 months.

• To thaw, let the frozen loaves stand, covered, at room temperature for 15 to 20 minutes.

• To heat, if desired, wrap in aluminum foil and place in a preheated 300°F oven until warm and softened, 1 to 2 minutes. Do not overheat or the crust will become dry and brittle.

Buying Pita

Once available only in specialty bakeries and gourmet delis, pita is now found in most supermarkets. Commercially baked pitas tend to be made of either unbleached all-purpose flour or whole-wheat flour and come in the following sizes:

Small: 4 to 4½ inches (about 1 ounce)

Medium or Regular: 5¾ to 6½ inches (about 2 ounces)

Large: 7¼ to 10 inches (about 3 ounces)

A1 BASIC PITA

Contrary to the standard method of allowing bread dough to rise before shaping, these loaves are *first* shaped and rolled, then allowed to rise before baking. This simplified version, which cuts preparation time by about 1½ to 2 hours, lets the yeast do its best work in the oven, thus assuring a better pocket. The result—a superior pita with a delightfully chewy, yet tender texture and a puff in every loaf!

2 cups warm water (90° to 110°F)
2 envelopes (¼ ounce each) active dry yeast
½ teaspoon sugar
2 teaspoons salt
5 to 5½ cups unbleached all-purpose flour, plus flour for kneading

1. Pour the water into a large bowl and sprinkle in the yeast. Stir to dissolve.

2. With a wooden spoon, stir the sugar and salt into the yeast mixture; mix thoroughly. Gradually add 5 cups of the flour, stirring constantly until the dough is smooth. Slowly work in the remaining flour (up to ½ cup) with your hands, kneading until the dough is no longer sticky. Turn the dough out onto a well-floured board. Knead until it is smooth and elastic, about 5 minutes.

3. Shape the dough into an even rectangle and cut it in half lengthwise. Divide the dough into 24 portions for small pitas; 12 for larger ones. Shape each portion into a smooth ball. Place the balls on a floured surface and cover them with slightly damp towels while you roll out 1 ball at a time.

4. Gently press each ball flat with your fingers, keeping it well rounded. Flour a work surface and a rolling pin. Roll each round from the center to the outer edge, giving the dough a ¼ turn after each roll, to form a perfect circle not quite ¼-inch thick (about 5 to 5½ inches in diameter for small pitas; about 8½ inches for larger ones). Carefully flip the circles over to smooth out any creases that might prevent the pocket from forming.

5. Fifteen minutes before the loaves have finished rising, preheat the oven to 500°F. At the same time, place an ungreased baking sheet in the oven to warm.

6. As each loaf is rolled, place it carefully on a floured surface and cover with a clean, dry towel; do not let the surface of the loaves dry out. Let the loaves rise in a warm draft-free area, 30 to 45 minutes.

7. To bake, place 4 small pitas or 1 large pita on the hot baking sheet. Bake on the bottom rack of the oven until puffed and lightly browned on the bottom and almost white on top, about 4 minutes for small pitas and about 3½ minutes for large; the pita will be soft and flexible. If desired, flip the loaves over after they have puffed and bake up to 1 minute longer to brown the tops; be careful not to let the pita get crisp and brittle.

8. Remove the hot pitas from the oven and wrap immediately in clean, dry towels until cool enough to handle. Serve warm or at room temperature. For information on storage and thawing, see page 19.

9. Repeat this process until all the pitas are baked.

Makes 24 small or 12 large pitas.

Variation *Poppy-Seed or Sesame Pita:* After rolling out each circle of dough in step 4, brush the tops lightly with water and sprinkle with poppy seeds or toasted sesame seeds, page 165. Let the loaves rise and bake as above.

PITA CROUTONS

Be cook-wise and penny smart! Save all those tops you cut off pitas that you fill. Make plain, cheese, or garlic croutons. They're wonderful in salads and especially good atop a bowl of soup!

4 cups pita scraps, cut in 1 to 1½-inch pieces
¼ cup butter
¼ cup olive oil

1. Preheat the oven to 375°F.

2. Melt the butter in the oil in a small saucepan over medium heat.

3. Spread the pita pieces in a baking pan. Pour the melted butter and oil over the top and toss gently to coat.

4. Bake in the oven, stirring occasionally, until lightly browned and crisp, about 15 to 20 minutes.

Makes 4 cups.

Variations *Garlic Croutons:*   Add 1 to 2 cloves of crushed garlic to the melted butter and oil.
Cheese Croutons: Sprinkle plain or garlic croutons with grated Parmesan cheese when you remove them from the oven and toss to coat evenly.

   To store, refrigerate in an airtight container for up to 1 month or freeze for up to 3 months.

WHOLE-WHEAT HONEY PITA

This recipe contains a mixture of whole-wheat and all-purpose flour to create a nutty-flavored pita. Whole-wheat flour is made from the ground kernels of whole wheat and contains all the bran and the wheat germ, as well as the starchy endosperm. The high gluten content of the all-purpose flour in combination with the whole-wheat flour helps to increase the dough's elasticity. This enables it to retain the bubbles of gas from the yeast, allowing it to rise or ''grow'' to its fullest and form a large pocket. Because wheat germ contains oil, whole-wheat flour will go rancid; if you don't use it very often, store it in the freezer.

2 cups whole-wheat flour
3½ cups unbleached all-purpose flour, plus flour for kneading
2 cups warm water (90° to 110°F)
2 envelopes (¼ ounce each) active dry yeast
1 tablespoon honey
1 teaspoon salt

1. Combine the whole-wheat and all-purpose flours in a large bowl; mix thoroughly. Set aside.

2. Pour the water into a second large bowl and sprinkle in the yeast. Stir to dissolve.

3. With a wooden spoon, stir the honey and salt into the yeast mixture; mix thoroughly. Gradually add 5 cups of the flour, stirring constantly, until the dough is smooth. Slowly work in the remaining flour (up to ½ cup) with your hands, kneading until the dough is no longer sticky. Turn the dough out onto a well-floured board. Knead until it is smooth and elastic, about 5 minutes.

4. Shape the dough into an even rectangle and cut it in half lengthwise. Divide the dough into 24 portions for small pitas; 12 for larger ones. Shape each portion into a smooth ball. Place the balls on a floured surface and cover them with slightly damp towels while you roll out 1 ball at a time.

5. Gently press each ball flat with your fingers, keeping it well rounded. Flour a work surface and rolling pin. Roll each round from the center to the outer edge, giving the dough a ¼ turn after each roll, to form a perfect circle not quite ¼-inch thick (about 5 to 5½ inches for small pitas; about 8½ inches for larger ones). Carefully flip the circles over to smooth out any creases that might prevent the pocket from forming.

6. As each loaf is rolled, place it carefully on a floured surface and cover with a clean, dry towel; do not let the surface of the loaves dry out. Let the loaves rise in a warm, draft-free area, 30 to 45 minutes.

7. Fifteen minutes before the loaves have finished rising, preheat the oven to 500°F. At the same time, place an ungreased baking sheet in the oven to preheat.

8. To bake, place 4 small pitas or 1

large pita on the hot baking sheet. Bake on the bottom rack of the oven until puffed and lightly browned on the bottom, about 4 minutes for small pitas and about 3½ minutes for large; the pita will be soft and flexible. If desired, flip the loaves over after they have puffed and bake up to 1 minute longer to brown the tops; be careful not to let the pita get crisp and brittle.

9. Remove the hot pitas from the oven and wrap immediately in clean, dry towels until cool enough to handle. Serve warm or at room temperature. For information on storage and thawing, see page 19.

10. Repeat this process until all the pitas are baked.

Makes 24 small or 12 large pitas.

Variations *Whole-Wheat Poppy-Seed or Sesame Pita:* After rolling out each circle of dough in Step 5, brush the tops lightly with water and sprinkle with poppy seeds or toasted sesame seeds, page 165. Let the loaves rise and bake as above.

Wheat-Germ Honey Pita: Wheat germ, the heart of the wheat kernel which is the part of the whole grain removed in the milling of white flour, imparts a grainy, nutty-flavored texture to pita. Remember to store wheat germ in the refrigerator once the package is opened.

½ cup regular wheat germ
5 cups unbleached, all-purpose
   flour
2 cups warm water (90° to 110°F)
2 envelopes (¼ ounce each) active
   dry yeast
1 tablespoon honey
2 teaspoons salt

1. Combine the wheat germ and all-purpose flour in a large bowl; mix thoroughly. Set aside.

2. Follow the directions from Step 2 of Whole-Wheat Honey Pita above.

Makes 24 small or 12 large pitas.

WHAT TO DO WITH PITAS
IF THEY DON'T PUFF

Check the Secrets to Baking Perfect Pita, page 18; perhaps the oven or the baking sheet is not as hot as it should be; perhaps there is a crease or a crack in the dough? No matter how perfect the dough or the technique, sometimes you'll find an occasional pita that will not puff as much as it should. Whatever you do, don't throw it away. Here are some clever uses for these errant loaves:

Make Breadsticks or Crisps   Preheat the oven to 400°F. Cut the pitas into strips and spread them with softened butter. Roll them in snipped chives, finely chopped nuts, poppy, caraway, or sesame seeds, or grated Parmesan cheese. Place on a baking sheet and bake until bubbly, 5 or 10 minutes. If you want crispy sticks, bake them longer. Make savory or sweet triangles using the seasonings for Pita Crisps, page 28.

Make Garlic Toast   Spread with softened butter seasoned with crushed garlic and broil until lightly browned and bubbly.

Make Plain, Cheese, or Garlic Croutons   Cut into 1-inch pieces and prepare croutons, page 22.

Make Bread Crumbs   Preheat the oven to 250°F. Tear the pitas into pieces, place them on a baking sheet, and bake until they are crisp and dry, but not browned. Or dry them at room temperature for several days until they are crisp. Place the crispy pieces in a blender or food processor fitted with the metal blade and process until fine and crumbly. Or place them in a paper bag and roll with a rolling pin until crumbly. To store, refrigerate in an airtight container for up to 1 month.

Make Pizzas   Toast one side until lightly browned. Turn the pita over and top with tomato sauce seasoned with oregano, garlic, and olive oil. Add a choice of your favorite ingredients such as mushrooms, pepperoni, green pepper, and onion. Sprinkle with grated mozzarella cheese and broil until hot and bubbly.

Make Bread Pudding   Cut into 1½-inch pieces and make Spiced Apple Pita Pudding with Vanilla Sauce, page 153.

Make Pocket Bread Salad   Tear pita into pieces and make Pocket Bread Salad (Fattoush), page 101.

Make Quick Zahter or Herbed Bread   Drizzle the loaves with olive oil, sprinkle with zahter or another favorite herb, and broil until hot and bubbly, 1 to 2 minutes.

HERBED ZAHTER PITA

Zahter is a piquant blend of herbs including thyme, marjoram, toasted sesame seeds, and sumac, the tart dried seeds of the sumac plant. Used throughout the Middle East, it is found only in Middle Eastern grocery stores in the United States. The tantalizing aroma of Zahter Pita in the oven is enough to break the resolutions of even the most serious dieter! Just as with Sweetened Sesame Pita, Herbed Zahter Pita does not puff because the herb mixture has been pressed into the dough.

1 recipe Basic Pita, page 21,
   prepared through step 2
¾ cup zahter
¾ cup olive oil

1. Shape the dough into an even rectangle and cut it in half lengthwise. Divide the dough into 12 portions. Shape each portion into a smooth ball. Place the balls on a floured surface and cover them with slightly damp towels to keep the surface of the dough supple and moist. Let the balls rise in a warm, draft-free place 30 to 45 minutes.

2. Fifteen minutes before the loaves have finished rising, preheat the oven to 425°F. Lightly grease a baking sheet.

3. Blend the zahter and the olive oil in a small bowl to make a thin paste. Set aside.

4. Working on 2 balls at a time and using your fingertips, gently press 2 balls flat, keeping them well rounded. Flour a work surface and rolling pin. Roll each round from the center to the outer edge to form a 7-inch circle.

5. Place the 2 rounds on the baking sheet. Spread the zahter paste evenly over the top of each round (1 tablespoon per round) pressing down with your fingertips to make the mixture stick.

6. Bake until the loaves are golden-brown and the seeds are toasted, 10 to 12 minutes. The bread should be soft not crisp. It will bake best if you bake 1 sheet at a time on an oven rack placed in the center or lower third of your oven. However, since this bread does not puff, if you wish to bake 2 sheets at a time, add another rack in the oven close to the first rack. Place 1 sheet on each rack, staggering 1 on the right and 1 on the left, and reverse the sheets from the top to bottom racks halfway through baking for even heat distribution.

7. Transfer to wire racks and let stand until cool enough to handle. Cut into wedges and serve warm or at room temperature. For information on storage and thawing, see page 19.

8. Repeat with the remaining dough, baking one batch before rolling and preparing the next.

Makes 12 loaves or 96 triangles.

SPICED ANISE TEA
(Shī Yensoon)

This exotic blend of spices join together to make a warm and tingly tea, perfect for a cold winter's afternoon or eve. Serve it with Pita Tea Sandwiches, page 49, or with Sweet Sesame Crisps, cheese, and fruit slices. On a hot day, offer it iced, topped with lemon slices and chopped walnuts.

6 cups water
3 cinnamon sticks, broken in half
3 to 4 whole cloves
2 inches fresh ginger, peeled and chopped
2 teaspoons anise seeds
Sugar or honey, to taste
Chopped walnuts (garnish)

Pour the water into a large saucepan and add the cinnamon, cloves, ginger, and anise seeds. Bring to a boil. Reduce the heat and simmer until the water tastes of the spices and turns brown from their color, 8 to 10 minutes. Stir in the sugar or honey to taste, or pass separately for optional use. Strain into teacups or glasses. Garnish each cup with a sprinkling of chopped walnuts.

Makes about 6 to 8 servings.

PITA TOAST

Pita makes heavenly toast. It's crisp and easy to handle.

Plain Toast: Split pitas into 2 rounds and toast (insides up) under the broiler. Use in place of melba toast.
Buttered Toast: Split pitas into 2 rounds and spread the insides with softened butter. Toast under the broiler until lightly browned. Serve with dips and pâtés or with smoked salmon or caviar.

PITA CRISPS

These fabulous crisps, adapted from a recipe of my good friend Delphine Wein of Boston, Massachusetts, are seasoned first then cut in wedges and baked to a light and crunchy crisp. I've created both savory and sweet varieties to be used in myriad ways.

SWEET CRISPS
Cinnamon Crisps: Preheat the oven to 325°F. Split pitas into 2 rounds and spread the insides with softened butter. Sprinkle with cinnamon and brown sugar. Cut into wedges and place on a baking sheet. Bake until crisp and lightly browned, about 10 to 15 minutes.
Sesame Crisps: Substitute sesame seeds for the cinnamon and follow the directions above.

SAVORY CRISPS
Preheat the oven to 325°F. Split pitas into 2 rounds and spread the insides with a mixture of softened butter and crushed garlic. Top with a choice of Parmesan cheese, poppy seeds, sesame seeds, oregano, or any other of your favorite seasonings.
Cut into wedges and place on a baking sheet. Bake until browned, about 10 to 15 minutes.
To store any of the above, cool and place in an airtight container. Refrigerate for up to 1 week or freeze for up to 3 months.

SWEETENED-SESAME PITA

Because you press sesame seeds into the dough in this recipe, these rounds will be flat, without the traditional pocket in the middle. The resulting pita have a delightfully chewy texture and sweet nutty flavor. Try them for dessert with fruit and cheese. They're guaranteed to bring raves when served with a glass of champagne.

1 recipe Basic Pita, page 21,
  prepared through step 2
¾ cup sugar
¼ to ⅓ cup cold water
1 cup sesame seeds

1. Shape the dough into an even rectangle and cut it in half lengthwise. Divide the dough into 12 portions. Shape each portion into a smooth ball. Place the balls on a floured surface and cover them with slightly damp towels to keep the surface of the dough supple and moist. Let the balls rest in a warm draft-free place 30 to 45 minutes.

2. Fifteen minutes before the loaves have finished rising, preheat the oven to 425°F. Lightly grease a baking sheet.

3. Blend the sugar with ¼ cup cold water in a small bowl to form a thick paste. Add up to ⅓ cup of water if necessary. Set aside.

4. Working on 2 balls at a time and using your fingertips, gently press each ball flat, keeping it well rounded. Flour a work surface and rolling pin. Roll out each round from the center to the outer edge to form a 7-inch circle.

5. Place the 2 rounds on the baking sheet. Spread the sugar paste evenly over the top of each round with your fingertips. Sprinkle each round with 4 teaspoons of sesame seeds, spreading them to the edges of the dough to coat evenly. Press down with your fingertips to make the seeds stick. Score each circle into 8 wedges, cutting completely through but leaving the wedges in place.

6. Bake until the loaves are golden-brown and the seeds are toasted, 10 to 12 minutes. The bread should be soft not crisp. The bread will bake best if you bake one sheet at a time on an oven rack placed in the center or lower third of your oven. However, since this bread does not puff, if you wish to bake 2 sheets at a time, add another rack in the oven close to the first rack. Place 1 sheet on each rack, staggering 1 on the right and 1 on the left, and reverse the sheets from the top to bottom racks halfway through baking for even heat distribution.

7. Separate the wedges and transfer to wire racks. Let stand until cool enough to handle.

8. Repeat with the remaining dough, baking one batch before rolling and preparing the next.

Makes 12 loaves or 96 triangles.

GRIDDLE-BAKED PITA PINWHEEL SANDWICHES

Spread each pita first with softened butter then with the chosen filling. Depending on the size of the wheel desired, stack anywhere from 2 to 4 rounds on top of each other. Roll up like a jelly roll. Seal the roll with softened butter then wrap it tightly with aluminum foil or plastic wrap. Refrigerate to chill, at least 1 hour. Cut into ¼-inch slices. Try any of the following fillings.

SAVORY
● Plain unsalted Yogurt Cheese, page 33, topped with thin slices of prosciutto. Place a thin dill pickle spear at one end of the top layer and roll from that end.
● Yogurt Cheese Spread mixed with chopped pimiento-stuffed olives, page 34.
● Gingered Fig Montrachet, page 71, topped with thin slices of country-cured ham.
● Yogurt Cheese Spread, mixed with finely chopped raw mushrooms, page 34, and topped with thinly sliced roast beef.
● Plain unsalted Yogurt Cheese, page 33, with thinly sliced smoked salmon topped with finely chopped capers. Place a marinated asparagus spear at one end of the top layer and roll from that end.
● Bulgur and Lamb Tartare, page 53, topped with finely chopped scallions and toasted pine nuts. Add a light sprinkling of crushed red pepper flakes.

SWEET
● Plain unsalted Yogurt Cheese, page 33, topped with a layer of finely chopped Spiced Glazed Figs, page 150.
● Plain unsalted Yogurt Cheese, page 33, sprinkled with cinnamon and brown sugar.
● Plain unsalted Yogurt Cheese, page 33, blended with crumbled halvah.
● Yogurt Cheese Spread mixed with blueberries or strawberries, page 34.

UNLEAVENED GRIDDLE-BAKED PITA

Wonderfully chewy and soft, this bread has no leavening agent and is ''baked'' on top of the range on a large griddle or skillet. Griddle-Baked Pita probably most resemble the first ancient loaves desert nomads baked for their supper. Use them to wrap around kebabs or to make dessert crêpes.

3 cups unbleached all-purpose flour or 2 cups all-purpose flour and 1 cup whole-wheat flour, plus flour for kneading
1 teaspoon salt
1 to 1½ cups warm water (90° to 110°F)
Vegetable oil

1. Combine the flour and salt in a large bowl. Stirring with a wooden spoon, add enough water so the dough pulls away from the sides of the bowl and is no longer sticky; stir until smooth.

2. Turn out onto a well-floured board and knead until the dough is smooth and elastic, 5 minutes.

3. Shape the dough into an even rectangle and cut it in half lengthwise. Divide the dough into 12 portions and shape into smooth balls. Cover with slightly damp towels and let rest about 5 to 10 minutes.

4. Gently press each ball flat with your fingers, keeping it well rounded. Flour a work surface and rolling pin. Roll out each round to form a 6- to 7-inch circle, or until almost paper thin. Cover each round with a slightly damp towel.

5. Lightly oil a griddle or large skillet and warm over medium-high heat until hot. Gently stretch each round as thin as possible without tearing as you place it on the griddle. Cook until browned, bubbly spots appear on the bottom, about 1½ minutes; turn and brown the other side. Remove from the griddle and immediately wrap in a clean towel until cool enough to handle. Serve warm or at room temperature. For information on storage and thawing, see page 19.

6. Repeat with the remaining dough until all the pitas are cooked. Lightly oil the griddle after cooking 3 or 4 loaves; do not add too much oil or the pitas will be soggy and heavy.

Makes 12 pitas.

HOMEMADE YOGURT
(Laban)

Yogurt, or *Laban* as it is called in Syria and Lebanon, is a staple in our household to enjoy as is, to use as an ingredient in many special dishes, or to make *Labani,* a fresh yogurt cheese. This is my husband Mitch's recipe, tried and tested to a creamy delight and low-calorie to boot, if you make it with 2% low-fat milk. The non-fat dry milk helps to add richness and body without adding fat.

¼ cup non-fat dry milk
1 quart whole or 2% low-fat milk
¼ cup plain yogurt starter (see note page 33)

1. Combine the non-fat dry milk and whole or 2% milk in a 2-quart saucepan. Stir until dissolved.

2. Heat the milk mixture over medium heat to 180°F or until bubbles begin to appear around the edges and a skin forms on top. Stir the skin into the mixture.

3. Remove from the heat and let cool to 120°F or until the milk feels comfortably warm to your little finger or when dropped on your wrist.

4. Put the yogurt starter in a small bowl and stir in about ½ cup of the lukewarm milk until the starter is completely dissolved. Add the yogurt mixure to the remaining lukewarm milk, stirring gently to blend.

5. Pour into individual glass containers or a 1-quart jar. Put the uncovered containers on a baking sheet in an unheated oven or cover them with clean dry towels and place in a warm, draft-free part of the kitchen. Let stand undisturbed until the yogurt is set, about 6 to 8 hours. The lower the percentage of fat in the milk, the longer the yogurt will take to set. And, the longer it sets, the more tart the yogurt.

6. To store, refrigerate, covered, for up to 1 week.

Makes 4 cups.

Secrets to Making Perfect Yogurt

• All utensils used in making and storing yogurt must be sterile.
• It is essential to use only very fresh whole or 2% low-fat milk.
• Check the temperature with a dairy thermometer or a built-in thermometer "spoon" available at houseware stores. In the days before our modern technology, testing the temperature was "by guess and by gosh," but it also works very well. If you can dip your little finger into the warm milk and count slowly to 10 without burning your finger the milk is ready.

Note: For your first batch of homemade yogurt, use plain commercial yogurt (look for one with no preservatives) as your starter. From then on, save at least ¼ cup from your last batch as the starter for your next. In the Middle East, they call this starter *rowbie*. In homes where large quantities of yogurt are made and consumed, it is possible that it could be a direct descendant from the last generation, from a grandmother, an aunt, or possibly a neighbor.

FRESH YOGURT CHEESE
(Labani)

This famous Middle Eastern cheese, called *Labani* (which means drained yogurt), has a delightfully piquant flavor and creamy texture. It is most often served for breakfast or as an appetizer with fresh pita. By adding different ingredients, yogurt cheese becomes a sweet or savory delicacy. Our favorite way of eating *Labani* is for breakfast, drizzled with olive oil, sprinkled with mint, and served with sliced tomatoes, cucumbers, and Calamata olives.

1 teaspoon salt, or more to taste
2 quarts plain yogurt, preferably homemade, page 32

1. At least one day before serving, gently stir the salt into the yogurt.

2. Line a colander with 4 single layers of cheesecloth. Pour the yogurt into the cheesecloth. Gather the corners into a bag and tie them together securely with a cord. Hang the bag over the kitchen faucet high enough to drain into the sink, or suspend over a deep bowl. (You may leave the yogurt to drain in the colander, however suspending it allows a better drain and results in a firmer, more creamy curd.) Let it drain overnight or until the yogurt curd is firm. The texture should be the consistency of softened cream cheese.

3. Remove from the bag and place in a container. To store, refrigerate, covered, for up to 1 week.

Makes about 1 quart (low-fat yogurt, because of its high water content, will yield a little less, about 3 pints).

Making Yogurt Cheese in a Commercial Container

Buy 1 quart of commercial yogurt and stir in ½ teaspoon salt. Pierce the bottom of the container in several places with a sharp fork. Place the container in a colander and let the yogurt drain until all the whey is removed and the curd in the container is firm and spreadable. Season as desired. Refrigerate, covered, for up to 1 week.

Savory Variations

Yogurt Cheese Spread:

1. In a medium bowl, season Yogurt Cheese, to taste, with crushed garlic; finely chopped pimiento-stuffed olives, raw mushrooms, or marinated sun-dried tomatoes; or minced herbs such as basil, dill, parsley, or mint. Blend gently until smooth. Depress the top of the cheese in several places with the back of a spoon. Refrigerate, covered, until firm, at least 30 minutes.

2. Drizzle with olive oil and serve as an appetizer spread surrounded with Basic Pita, page 21, cut into wedges.

Yogurt Cheese Balls or Logs:

1. Divide the prepared cheese into 2 large or 12 small portions.

2. Place each portion on a double fold of cheesecloth and shape into a ball or log. Refrigerate, covered, until firm, at least 30 minutes.

3. Remove the cheesecloth and roll in any of the following: finely chopped parsley, freshly ground black pepper, finely chopped fresh mint, or crumbled dried mint. Drizzle with olive oil and serve with Herbed Zahter Pita, page 26, cut into wedges.

Sweet Variations

Yogurt Cheese Spread:

1. Omit the salt when making Yogurt Cheese.

2. Place the cheese in a medium bowl and add finely chopped raisins, dates, blueberries, or strawberries, to taste. Blend gently until smooth. Refrigerate, covered, until firm, at least 30 minutes. Serve as a breakfast spread or a dessert-cheese spread with Pita Toast, page 28.

Yogurt Cheese Balls or Logs:

1. Divide the unsalted cheese into balls or logs as directed in Savory Yogurt Cheese, above. Refrigerate, covered, until firm, at least 30 minutes.

2. Remove the cheesecloth and roll in any of the following: finely chopped honeyed peanuts, finely minced raisins, or a cinnamon-sugar blend.

3. Serve as a brunch confection or for afternoon tea with Sweet Sesame Crisps, page 28.

Other Ways For Draining Yogurt to Make Yogurt Cheese

• Use a commercial yogurt maker with an attachment for draining the yogurt to make yogurt cheese.

• Stitch together a muslin bag with a drawstring large enough to hold a quart of homemade yogurt. Make the drawstring long enough to tie on a kitchen faucet or to use with some other method of suspension. (A photographer friend suspends his yogurt bags from a tripod.)

• Reserve a new white, thin cotton sock for draining yogurt.

• Set aside a new large linen or cotton handkerchief to line a colander.

• Cut an old but clean cotton T-shirt large enough to line a colander or strainer.

• Buy a large flannel filter used for making Latin coffees and suspend its frame over a jar or small bowl to fit.

WHITE CHEESE
(Jiban)

Jiban, which means
"cheese" in Arabic,
is an easy to make
fresh white cheese
curd, which is either
creamy or firm, de-
pending on how much
moisture is removed.

   This version is a
fresh natural product
thickened into curds
with yogurt and lemon
juice. It is then
drained, kneaded to a
smooth texture, sea-
soned, shaped, tied
into cheesecloth, and
marinated in garlicky
olive oil. Or, if you
like, you can make a
feta-like cheese by re-
moving more moisture,
forming it into patties,
and marinating it in
it's own salted whey.
(See variation below.)

½ gallon whole milk
1 cup yogurt, preferably
   homemade, see page 32
1 tablespoon plus 1 teaspoon fresh
   lemon juice
Salt, to taste
Optional ingredients (see below)
½ cup olive oil
2 peeled garlic cloves, cut in half

Optional Ingredients

2 tablespoons finely chopped black
   Greek or green olives, squeezed in
   a towel to remove excess moisture.
2 tablespoons any favorite finely
   chopped fresh herb such as
   cilantro, chives, or dill or 1
   tablespoon finely chopped fresh
   basil
1 tablespoon, or more to taste,
   finely chopped green chiles
Freshly ground black pepper or
   cayenne, to taste

1.   Heat the milk in a large kettle or
saucepan over medium-high heat,
stirring occasionally, until it comes
to a full boil, about 15 to 20 minutes.

2.   Stir in the yogurt and blend
thoroughly. Add the lemon juice
and boil about 1½ minutes longer,
without stirring until the curd sepa-

rates from the yellowish whey. The
milk will foam as it boils.

3.   Remove the milk-yogurt mixture from the heat and cool to lukewarm, about 15 minutes.

4.   Line a colander with 4 single
layers of cheesecloth. Pour the
curds and whey into the colander.
(Reserve the whey if you wish to
make a feta-like cheese.)

5.   Let the cheese drain until most
of the moisture is removed, about
20 minutes. (It is important to leave
some moisture in the curds to aid in
the kneading process and to give the
cheese a creamy smooth texture.)
Bring the corners of the cheesecloth
together and squeeze the cheese until it is soft, yet firm.

6.   Remove the cheesecloth and
place the cheese on a large platter.
Salt to taste and knead it with your
fingers until the texture is smooth,
about 3 to 5 minutes. Add any optional ingredients, if desired.

7.   Shape the cheese into 1 x 2½-
inch patties. Tie each patty in a
square of double-thickness cheesecloth to hold the curds firmly together. Place them in a glass or plastic refrigerator dish and add the oil

and garlic cloves. Cover and marinate in the refrigerator, turning the cheese occasionally, for at least 2 hours before serving.

8. Remove from the refrigerator an hour before serving to bring out the full flavor of the cheese.

9. To store, refrigerate, covered, for up to 1 week, adding more oil, if necessary, to keep the cheese moist.

Makes 8 patties.

Variation *Feta-like Cheese:*
1. Reserve the whey as it is drained from the curds. See step 4 above. Season it with salt (3 cups of whey to 2 tablespoons salt).

2. Remove most of the moisture from the curds, leaving just enough to mold and shape the cheese into firm, smooth patties. Salt the cheese, if desired, and shape into 2 large or 4 small patties. It is not necessary to wrap the patties in cheesecloth as above.

3. Cover and store the cheese in the whey-brine solution in the refrigerator for up to 2 weeks.

Lazy Mediterranean Breakfasts

1. Apricot nectar
Minted Yogurt Cheese drizzled
   with olive oil
Herbed Zahter Pitas
Tomato and Onion Salad
Cucumber slices and
   marinated black Greek
   olives
Buttered Basic Pita
Baked Ruby Quince with
   Walnuts
Coffee or Tea

2. Orange Yogurt Shake
Fresh purple Black Mission figs
Herb-Scrambled Eggs in
   Yogurt-Cheese-Spread
   Poppy-Seed Pitas
Thinly sliced minted tomatoes
Coffee or Tea

3. Peach Yogurt Shake
Sliced oranges with orange-
   blossom syrup
Capered Smoked Salmon and
   Cheese with buttered Pita
   Toast
Whipped Sweet Butter and
   fresh homemade preserves
Griddle-Baked Pitas
Coffee or Tea

PICKER UPPERS

A Picker Upper is an appetizer, a snack, an hors d'oeuvre, a tid-bit—whatever you label it, it is fabulous finger food.

Translating the Picker-Upper into Middle Eastern hospitality is to explain the *meze*, the Arabic version of Western cocktails with hors d'oeuvres. The *meze*, served at the beginning of a meal, might be a simple bowl of olives and a crock of yogurt cheese served with pita. Or, more likely, it is a lavish spread with a range of dips, tarts, triangles, pies, and crudités plus a liberal supply of warm pitas which scoop up everything so well. The *meze* is a celebration in its own right and best describes the very essence of Middle Eastern hospitality, an opportunity to "break bread" with friends, a time for easy conversation and good food. In the center of it all is pita—baskets full of wedges, crisps, and soft little loaves that work so well with this fare—for pita is not only a bread but an essential eating tool.

T he dishes are piquant, tangy, and earthy. Most of them can be prepared in advance and presented with very little last-minute fuss which works perfectly for casual American lifestyles. Try my Middle-Eastern classics such as *Baba Ghanouge,* and Pita Pyramids and dabble with all the other unusual dishes I've included such as Open-Faced Goat Cheese Pita Tarts. Pita is the definitive *picker upper.*

HUMMUS BI TAHINI
(Chickpea Purée)

Hummus Bi Tahini is perhaps the most well known of all the Middle Eastern appetizers. A purée of chickpeas seasoned with Tahini, lemon juice, and garlic, *Hummus* is at once a dip, a spread, a pita filling, or a sandwich topping. Here I've added lots of lemon juice to enliven the subtle flavors. If you like a more spicy *hummus* add cayenne pepper to taste, or serve crushed red pepper flakes as an accompaniment. Or, try using a little cumin for a more exotic variation. While I've given you a choice of using either canned or dried chickpeas, the dried peas have a more natural, nutty taste.

¼ cup tahini (sesame seed paste; recipe follows)
⅓ cup fresh lemon juice
⅓ to ½ cup warm water
1 clove garlic, chopped
¾ cup dried chickpeas (garbanzo beans), cooked and drained (see note) or 2 cups (1-pound can) chickpeas, drained and rinsed
½ teaspoon salt
Freshly ground black pepper, to taste
Olive oil (garnish)
Chopped fresh parsley (garnish)
Whole-Wheat Honey Pitas, page 23, cut into wedges

1. Put the tahini, lemon juice, water, and garlic into a blender or a food processor fitted with the metal blade. Cover and process until smooth.

2. With the machine running, gradually add the chickpeas, salt, and pepper, processing until the mixture is the consistency of a very thick paste. If necessary, stop the machine and scrape down the sides with a spatula. The mixture will thicken when it is refrigerated, so if it seems too thick when you've finished processing it, add up to ½ cup more water and process again. Taste to correct seasonings.

3. Put the *hummus* into a bowl and refrigerate, covered, to chill. Before serving, drizzle with olive oil and garnish with the chopped parsley. Surround with freshly made pita wedges.

To store, refrigerate, covered, for up to 1 week, or freeze for up to 3 months.

Makes 2 cups.

Note: To cook dried chickpeas, put ¾ cup dried chickpeas in a medium bowl, cover with water almost to the top of the bowl, and soak overnight. Drain, put in a saucepan, and cover with fresh water. Cover and bring to a boil, reduce heat, and cook until soft, about 1 hour. Drain and cool. Makes 2 cups cooked chickpeas.

HOMEMADE TAHINI
(Sesame Seed Paste)

While Tahini is readily available in health food stores, Middle Eastern groceries, and even most supermarkets today, it is also very easy to make your own.

4 cups sesame seeds
¼ to ½ cup vegetable oil

1. Preheat the oven to 350°F.

2. Spread the sesame seeds on a shallow baking tray and bake, shaking frequently, until fragrant, 8 to 10 minutes. Do not brown. Cool.

3. Put the sesame seeds in a blender or food processor fitted with the metal blade. Add the vegetable oil. Process to a smooth paste, about 5 minutes. Add more oil if necessary, to bring the paste to a thick pouring consistency. Tahini will keep stored in a tightly covered jar in the refrigerator for several months.

Makes 3 cups.

HUMMUS GUACAMOLE

For today's eclectic palates, here is a combination of *Hummus Bi Tahini* and Mexican guacamole. Oven-baked pita crisps make marvelous accompaniments instead of the usual tortilla chips. The lemon juice in the *Hummus* complements the subtle flavor of the avocado and helps it to retain its natural color.

1 ripe avocado, peeled
1 recipe Hummus Bi Tahini,
*   page 40*
1 scallion, finely chopped
1 small ripe tomato, finely chopped
1 tablespoon finely chopped hot
*   green chiles*
Olive oil (garnish)
Chopped fresh cilantro (garnish)
Parmesan Pita Crisps, page 28

1. Scoop the avocado into a medium bowl and mash with a fork. Add the *hummus bi tahini* and blend thoroughly.

2. Gently stir in the scallion, tomato, and chiles. Taste to correct seasonings. You may want to add more fresh lemon juice, garlic, salt, and pepper, than is called for in the recipe for *hummus bi tahini.*

3. Put the dip into a serving dish and refrigerate, covered, to chill. Before serving, drizzle with olive oil and garnish with chopped cilantro. Offer plenty of Parmesan pita crisps for scooping up this dip.

4. To store, follow the directions for *hummus bi tahini.*

Makes 3 cups.

HOT HUMMUS AND FETA CHEESE

Serving *Hummus Bi Tahini* hot with feta cheese and chiles adds a whole new dimension to this versatile dip. While it is sensational with warm pita wedges or pita toast, it is equally good with cool, crunchy crudités.

1 recipe Hummus Bi Tahini,
    page 40
3 scallions, chopped
⅔ cup crumbled feta cheese
½ cup finely chopped fresh cilantro
1 to 2 teaspoons mild chili powder
2 tablespoons olive oil
Finely chopped scallions (garnish)
Sesame Pita Crisps, page 28

1. Put the *hummus* in a medium bowl and fold in the scallions, feta cheese, cilantro, and chili powder. Blend thoroughly. Taste to correct seasonings.

2. Heat the olive oil in a chafing dish. Add the seasoned *hummus* and stir until the mixture is hot and bubbly, about 5 to 10 minutes.

3. Serve warm in the chafing dish garnished with the chopped scallions. Surround with pita crisps.

4. To store, refrigerate, covered, for up to 1 week.

Makes about 3 cups.

A Middle-Eastern *Meze* Spread

Baskets of freshly baked Basic, Whole-Wheat Honey, and Griddle-Baked Pitas
Crudités: celery and cucumber sticks, radishes, tomato wedges
Yogurt Cheese Ball rolled in parsley and drizzled with olive oil
Hummus Bi Tahini
Baba Ghanouge
Piquant Pickled Turnips
Bulgur and Lamb Tartare
Marinated Artichokes with Salonika Peppers
Fried Eggplant and Squash with Taratour
Fluted Pita Meat Pies
Tabbouleh
Pistachio Nuts
Fresh fruit in season: figs, persimmons, pomegranates, apricots
Turkish Coffee

HERBED HUMMUS WITH PISTACHIOS

This unorthodox yet interesting variation on a *hummus* theme adds a welcome contrast of flavor and texture. The pungent taste of freshly chopped watercress and cilantro and the crunchiness of the pistachios meld together to bring out the nuttiness of the puréed chickpeas. After sampling this recipe, perhaps you will be inspired to try your own favorite combinations of fresh herbs and nuts with *hummus*.

1 recipe Hummus Bi Tahini, page 40
½ cup finely chopped watercress
½ cup finely chopped fresh cilantro
½ cup chopped pistachio nuts
Olive oil (garnish)
Pistachio nuts (garnish)
Poppy-Seed Pitas, page 22, cut into wedges

1. Put the *hummus* in a medium bowl and fold in the watercress and cilantro. Blend thoroughly. Taste to correct seasonings. Refrigerate, covered, to chill.

2. Add the chopped pistachio nuts and mix thoroughly. Turn into a serving dish and drizzle with olive oil. Garnish with the additional nuts. Serve with poppy-seed pita wedges.

3. To store, follow the directions for *hummus bi tahini*, page 40.

Makes about 2½ to 3 cups.

BABA GHANOUGE
(Eggplant Sesame Purée)

This sharp smoky purée of eggplant and Tahini blended with just the right amount of lemon juice and freshly crushed garlic is redolent of the flavors of the Middle East. Translated literally, *Baba Ghanouge* means "pampered father" or "spoiled father," a phrase, no doubt, coined long ago by loving wives anxious to coddle their beloved husbands or fathers. Now, pamper yourself and your guests with this version. Chances are, you'll come up with some of your own variations, too. Serve it as a dip for scooping with pita wedges or as a filling for a pita sandwich!

1 large (about 1½ pounds) eggplant
¼ cup tahini (sesame seed paste) page 41
¼ cup warm water
3 tablespoons fresh lemon juice, or more, to taste
1 clove garlic, crushed
Salt and freshly ground black pepper, to taste
Olive oil (garnish)
Parsley sprigs (garnish)
Wheat-Germ Honey Pitas, page 24, cut into wedges

1. Preheat the broiler.

2. Pierce one side of the eggplant with a fork. Place, pierced side up, on a foil-covered broiler pan set on a rack so that the top of the eggplant is about 5 or 6 inches from the heat source. Broil until the top is charred and starts to blister and the bottom is soft to the touch, about 30 to 45 minutes.

3. Remove and let cool until the eggplant can be handled easily, about 10 minutes. Slit the softened side and scoop the pulp into a medium bowl, scraping all the flesh from the inner skin. Pour off any darkened liquid and remove any large cluster of seeds as both may impart an unpleasant bitter taste. Mash the pulp well with a fork.

4. Mix the tahini with the warm water until smooth and whitened. Add the mixture to the eggplant along with the lemon juice, garlic, salt, and pepper. Mix until pale in color and smooth. Taste to correct seasonings.

5. Transfer to a serving bowl, and refrigerate, covered, to chill. Before serving, drizzle with olive oil and garnish with parsley. Serve with wheat-germ honey pita wedges.

6. To store, follow the directions for *hummus bi tahini*, page 40.

Makes about 2 cups.

Variation *Eggplant Caviar:* Omit the tahini and water. Add 3 finely chopped scallions and 2 tablespoons olive oil to the remaining ingredients and follow the directions above. You may add other chopped vegetables such as tomatoes or green pepper. Taste to correct seasonings. Refrigerate, covered, to chill.

Selecting and Preparing Eggplant

Select eggplants that are firm, heavy for their size, cylindrical in shape, smooth, and glossy. While the royal dark-purple variety is the most commonly available, eggplants also come in white, reddish, and yellowish tints, and even in a mottled stripe.

Eggplants are characteristically porous and contain a lot of water which can make them bitter. Depending upon the recipe to be prepared, there are several things you can do to avoid this bitterness.

● If you're broiling eggplant, pour off the darkened liquid that collects.

● If you're frying or baking, first slice the eggplant and layer the slices on paper towels, lightly salting each side as you layer the eggplant. Cover the top with another layer of paper towels, pat down lightly and let the eggplant stand for about an hour to remove the excess moisture. Then pat the eggplant slices completely dry with fresh paper towels.

OLIVE-LACED BABA GHANOUGE

In this recipe, the eggplant-tahini blend is especially distinctive with the addition of olives and *zahter,* an herb blend of marjoram, thyme, toasted sesame seeds, and sumac.

1 recipe Baba Ghanouge, page 44
1 cup pitted and finely chopped black Greek olives
½ to 1 teaspoon zahter (see page 166 for a substitute)
Olive oil (garnish)
Chopped fresh parsley (garnish)
Basic Pitas, page 21, cut into wedges

1. Put the *baba ghanouge* in a medium bowl and fold in the chopped olives and *zahter*. Blend thoroughly. Taste to correct seasonings.

2. Transfer to a serving dish and refrigerate, covered, to chill. Before serving, drizzle with olive oil and garnish with chopped parsley. Serve with the pita wedges.

To store, follow the directions for *hummus bi tahini*, page 40.

Makes about 3 cups.

CHICKEN LIVER PATE

Crispy toasted pita wedges are perfect for scooping up this unusual Chicken Liver Pâté. The classic French appetizer boasts a Mediterranean twist with a hefty measure of anchovy paste and Yogurt Cheese.

2 tablespoons plus ½ cup (1 stick) softened butter
2 pounds chicken livers
½ cup (1 medium) chopped onion
½ cup Cognac
⅓ cup firm Yogurt Cheese, page 33
3 tablespoons anchovy paste
½ teaspoon salt
½ teaspoon crumbled dried thyme
½ cup finely chopped fresh parsley
2 hard-cooked eggs, yolks and whites sieved separately (garnish)
Plain Pita Toast, page 28

1. Melt the 2 tablespoons of butter in a heavy skillet. Add the chicken livers and onion and sauté over medium heat, stirring frequently, until the livers are brown on the outside but still pink inside, 5 minutes.

2. With a slotted spoon, remove the livers and onions to a blender or food processor fitted with the metal blade. Reduce the remaining juices in the skillet by half and add to the chicken livers.

3. Heat the Cognac in a small saucepan over medium heat until reduced to ¼ cup; be careful not to let it ignite. Add it to the livers. Add the remaining butter, yogurt cheese, anchovy paste, salt, and thyme. Process the mixture until completely blended and smooth. Transfer to a bowl and refrigerate, covered, until firm.

4. Divide the pâté in half. Shape each half into a cylinder and roll both in the chopped parsley to coat. Place the pâté rolls on a platter and garnish with the sieved egg yolks and whites. Serve with pita toast.

Makes two 6 x 2½-inch logs.

An Elegant Cocktail Party

Buttered Pita Toast
Capered Smoked Salmon and Cheese
Caviar surrounded by lemon wedges, chopped hard-cooked egg, and chopped sweet onion
Chicken Liver Pâté
Chilled Champagne

ORIENTAL SHRIMP AND BLACK BEAN DIP

Everytime I go to our favorite Chinese restaurant in New York's Chinatown, I ask the chef to create a special version of Shrimp and Black Bean Sauce. I always insist that he sliver the ginger and sprinkle it generously with finely chopped scallions which perfectly complement the flavors of the shrimp and black bean sauce. One day I decided to use these ingredients as a dip in combination with creamy Yogurt Cheese. Here I use plain black beans rather than the fermented Chinese variety, which would overpower the delightful tanginess of the Yogurt Cheese.

1 recipe Yogurt Cheese, page 33
1 pound cooked medium shrimp
¼ cup dried black beans, cooked, (see note) or ½ cup canned black beans, heated
3 scallions, finely chopped
1 teaspoon finely slivered fresh ginger
1 clove garlic, crushed
½ to 1 teaspoon soy sauce
Salt and freshly ground black pepper, to taste
Chopped scallions (garnish)
Whole-Wheat Honey Pitas, page 23, cut into wedges

1.   Combine all the ingredients except the scallions for garnish and pita wedges in a medium bowl. Mix thoroughly and taste to correct seasonings. Refrigerate, covered, to chill.

2.   Transfer the dip to a serving bowl and garnish with the chopped scallions. Serve with warm whole-wheat pita wedges.

Makes about 3½ cups.

Note: Cook black beans by first rinsing them in cold running water and discarding any stones or shriveled beans. Cover each 1 cup of dry beans with 3 cups of water and let stand for 12 hours or overnight. Cook the beans in the water they have soaked in until they are tender, about 1 to 1½ hours. The beans should be soft, yet firm, not mushy. Soak the ¼ cup of dry beans called for in this recipe in just under 1 cup of water for at least 12 hours. Cook as above; they should be ready in 35 to 45 minutes.

How to Cook Shrimp

Bring a large saucepan of water to a boil. Add a few parsley sprigs, peppercorns, 2 small bay leaves, and a dash of salt. Add the shrimp and bring the water back to boiling. Immediately reduce the heat to low and simmer until the shrimp is a delicate pink, 2 to 3 minutes. To ensure that the shrimp will be tender, never overcook them and never cook them over high heat. Drain and refrigerate to chill. (Do not plunge the shrimp into ice water to chill as this will make them tough and waterlogged.) Shell and devein.

TARAMOSALATA
(Greek Fish Roe Salad)

Tart and tangy, this dip is a superb addition to a Middle Eastern *meze* spread. Don't forget to serve some juicy black Greek olives accompanied by cucumber and celery strips for dipping. Buttered pita toast ties everything together.

3 slices white bread, crusts removed
3 tablespoons water
6 tablespoons carp or cod roe
2 tablespoons minced onion
¾ cup olive oil
3 tablespoons fresh lemon juice
1 small clove garlic (optional)
Chopped fresh parsley (garnish)
Buttered Pita Toast, page 28
Black Greek olives
Celery and cucumber strips

1. Sprinkle the bread with the water to soften, then squeeze dry.

2. Place the bread, roe, onion, ¼ cup oil, lemon juice, and garlic in a blender and blend until smooth.

3. With the machine running, add the remaining oil in a slow steady stream. Continue blending until the mixture is creamy.

4. Put the dip into a bowl and refrigerate, covered, to chill. Before serving, garnish with the chopped parsley. Surround with the buttered pita toast, black Greek olives, and celery and cucumber strips.

Makes about 1½ cups.

CAPERED SMOKED SALMON

This pastel-colored spread of salmon and capers is given a Middle Eastern accent with the use of Yogurt Cheese as a base. It is a special treat with crisp Buttered Pita Toast and a glass or two of Champagne.

1 recipe Yogurt Cheese, page 33 (omit the salt)
⅔ cup smoked salmon, cut into julienne strips
2 scallions, finely chopped
1 teaspoon fresh lemon juice
1 to 2 tablespoons capers, finely chopped, to taste
Freshly ground black pepper, to taste
Lemon wedges (garnish)
Buttered Pita Toast, page 28

1. Combine all the ingredients except the lemon wedges and pita toast in a medium bowl. Mix gently until smooth; taste to correct seasonings. Refrigerate, covered, to chill.

2. Transfer to a serving bowl. Garnish with the lemon wedges and surround with buttered pita toast.

Makes about 3 cups.

PITA TEA SANDWICHES

For an unusual tea party, offer pots of freshly brewed Mint Tea, page 158, and Spiced Anise Tea, page 27, and a tray of dainty pita tea sandwiches. Pitas filled with a choice of savory and sweet fillings are perfect for the occasion. Cut large pitas into triangles. Spread them first with Yogurt Cheese, and add an array of enticing fillings. (For the sweet or fruity varieties, use unsalted Yogurt Cheese.)

- Sliced avocado and chopped scallions
- Cucumber and smoked salmon
- Watercress sprigs and sliced hard-cooked egg
- Cilantro sprigs and tiny boiled shrimp
- Capers and smoked turkey
- Arugula and smoked ham
- Chopped black Greek olives
- Marinated sun-dried tomatoes sprinkled with chopped fresh basil
- Sliced radishes and shrimp or lobster salad
- Flaked crabmeat and sliced papaya
- Homemade red raspberry or blackberry preserves
- Sliced strawberries or peaches
- Chopped raisins or dates and pecans
- Chopped dried or sliced fresh figs and thinly sliced orange

If you make the sandwiches ahead, top them with a very lightly dampened double-thickness of paper towels and wrap in aluminum foil or transparent plastic wrap. Store in the refrigerator to chill. To serve, arrange them on a tray and offer at room temperature for peak flavor.

SHRIMP WITH AVOCADO-SESAME SAUCE

This shrimp dressed in a lemony avocado-sesame sauce is quite different—tart and nutty with a decided taste of the sea. Serve it as an appetizer accompanied by soft fresh pita wedges or use it as a filling for a lettuce-lined pita pocket topped with thinly sliced tomato. Save a little dressing to drizzle on top!

1 medium ripe avocado, peeled and mashed
3 tablespoons tahini (sesame seed paste), page 41
1 clove garlic, crushed
¼ cup fresh lemon juice or more, to taste
Salt and freshly ground black pepper, to taste
2 to 4 tablespoons water
½ cup finely chopped fresh parsley
1½ pounds cooked medium shrimp
Whole-Wheat Sesame Pitas, page 24, cut into wedges

1. Mix the avocado, tahini, garlic, lemon juice, salt, and pepper in a large bowl; add water gradually (up to 4 tablespoons) until the mixture is of a thick pouring consistency. Taste to correct seasonings.

2. Blend in the chopped parsley. Add the shrimp and toss gently to coat. Refrigerate, covered, to chill.

3. Place on a serving platter and surround with whole-wheat sesame pita wedges.

Makes 6 to 8 servings.

Backyard Barbecue

Olive-Laced Baba Ghanouge with Basic Pita wedges
Shrimp with Avocado-Sesame Sauce and Whole-Wheat Sesame Pita wedges
Yogurt-Marinated Shish Kebabs in Basic Pitas
Herb-Broiled Chicken and Onion on Herbed Zahter Pitas
Minted Potato Salad
Classic Mediterranean Salad
Pita and Halvah
Iced beer
Coffee

KIBBEH
(Middle-Eastern Meatballs)

The recipe that follows is a basic mixture for cooked *Kibbeh*. This varies slightly from Bulgur and Lamb Tartare (*Kibbeh Nayee*) in that I've included ⅓ cup less bulgur per pound of ground meat so that the cooked dish has a firmer texture for eating out of hand. The first time you serve these little nuggets of goodness you'll find they'll be devoured like popcorn and your guests will come back for more!

⅔ cup fine-grade bulgur
1 pound ground lean lamb (all fat removed)
1 small onion, grated
¼ teaspoon ground allspice
¼ teaspoon ground cinnamon
Salt and freshly ground black pepper, to taste
Vegetable oil, for frying
Basic Pitas, page 21, cut into wedges
Yogurt-Garlic Sauce (recipe below)

1. Rinse the bulgur and place it in a medium bowl. Cover with cool water and let soak until it is tender to the bite, 20 to 30 minutes. Drain thoroughly and squeeze out any excess water. Fluff to separate the grains.

2. Combine the lamb, onion, allspice, cinnamon, salt, and pepper in a large bowl. Mix thoroughly.

3. Prepare a bowl of ice and water. Keeping your hands cold and moist by dipping them into the bowl of ice and water, gradually add the

About Kibbeh

Kibbeh is the national dish of both Lebanon and Syria. This distinctive and healthful combination of finely ground lean lamb, bulgur, onions, and spices is the basis of many wonderful dishes that star with pita. These dishes are made into various shapes and sizes, are filled or layered, then fried, baked, or even eaten raw, much like steak tartare. Ask your butcher to grind lean meat very fine or, if you wish, you may do it in your food processor or meat grinder. I have included all the popular *kibbeh* recipes that complement pita and that are always found on a *meze* spread. With the exception of Bulgur and Lamb Tartare (*Kibbeh Nayee*), all these *kibbeh* dishes may be made ahead and refrigerated, covered, for up to 3 days or frozen for up to 3 months. To serve, thaw in the refrigerator overnight. Reheat in a preheated 325°F oven until warmed through, about 10 to 15 minutes.

bulgur to the lamb mixture, kneading thoroughly after each addition. Knead the mixture for another minute after all the bulgur has been added. Taste to correct seasonings.

4. Divide the *kibbeh* into 36 portions and shape into smooth balls. Refrigerate the balls, covered, in a large bowl until firm, 30 minutes to 1 hour.

5. Pour the oil to a depth of ½ inch in a large skillet and heat until hot but not smoking. Working in batches add the meatballs in a single layer and cook over medium-high heat, turning often until evenly browned and cooked through, 5 to 8 minutes. Drain on paper towels. Add more oil to the skillet, if necessary, to cook the remaining meatballs.

6. Serve warm with pita wedges and a bowl of yogurt-garlic sauce for dipping.

Makes 3 dozen meatballs.

YOGURT-GARLIC SAUCE

Yogurt-Garlic Sauce is an especially versatile sauce which goes equally well with meat, fish, and vegetables. Use it both as a dip or as a dressing for pita sandwiches.

1 cup plain yogurt, preferably homemade, page 32
1 clove garlic, crushed
1 teaspoon fresh lemon juice
1 tablespoon finely chopped fresh parsley
Salt and freshly ground black pepper, to taste

Combine all the ingredients in a small bowl and stir gently to blend. Refrigerate, covered, to chill.

Makes 1 cup.

Variations
Yogurt-Mint Sauce: Substitute 1 tablespoon chopped fresh mint or 1 teaspoon crumbled dried mint for the parsley.

Yogurt-Cucumber Sauce: Add ½ cup finely chopped cucumber to the main recipe.

BULGUR AND LAMB TARTARE
(Kibbeh Nayee)

Translated literally, *Kibbeh Nayee* means naked or raw *kibbeh*. Rather like a rough-textured steak tartare, *Kibbeh Nayee* is always found on the *meze* or appetizer tray in a Middle Eastern home or restaurant. In order to savor the fresh taste of the lamb and bulgur, I rarely season this version with anything more than salt and pepper, although I've suggested an optional measure of cinnamon or allspice. Offer freshly cracked black pepper or crushed red pepper flakes as an accompaniment as well as a cruet of fruity olive oil. Soft pita wedges are a must.

1 cup fine- or medium-grade bulgur
1 pound ground lean lamb (all fat removed)
⅓ cup (about ⅓ large) grated sweet onion
Salt and pepper, to taste
Ground allspice or cinnamon, to taste (optional)
1 to 2 tablespoons ice water
Olive oil (garnish)

Chopped fresh parsley or mint (garnish)
Basic Pitas, page 21, cut into wedges

1. Rinse the bulgur and place it in a medium bowl. Cover with cool water and let soak until it is tender to the bite, 20 to 30 minutes. Drain thoroughly and squeeze out any ex-

Presentation for Bulgur and Lamb Tartare

It is true that we begin every dining experience with our eyes and with Bulgur and Lamb Tartare (*Kibbeh Nayee*) there is no exception. Try experimenting with these and other presentations. Always offer pita wedges as an accompaniment, of course, along with a cruet of olive oil, a dish of crushed red pepper flakes, and a pepper mill.

● Grease a small loaf pan or mold with olive oil and firmly press the chilled *Kibbeh Nayee* into the pan. Turn it over to unmold and place it on a serving platter or cutting board. Garnish with chopped crisp scallions and toasted pine nuts. Offer a knife or pie server and suggest guests slice into ½-inch servings.

● Shape into orange-size balls and roll them in finely chopped parsley or a light sprinkling of freshly cracked black peppercorns. Serve them on a lettuce-lined crystal platter with a spoon or cheese spreader.

● Shape into individual walnut-size balls and mound them on a serving platter. Garnish with finely chopped parsley and scallions. Drizzle with olive oil.

cess water. Fluff to separate the grains.

2.   Combine the lamb, onion, salt, pepper, and allspice or cinnamon in a large bowl. Mix thoroughly.

3.   Prepare a bowl of ice and water. Keeping your hands cold and moist by dipping them into the bowl of ice and water, gradually add the bulgur to the lamb mixture, kneading thoroughly after each addition. Add 1 to 2 tablespoons of the ice water to the mixture and continue kneading until it is slightly softened. Taste to correct seasonings.

4.   Shape the *kibbeh nayee* into a mound on a serving platter. Refrig-

erate, covered, for at least 1 hour. Depress a pattern on the surface with the tines of a fork; drizzle with olive oil and garnish with fresh parsley or mint. Serve with fresh pita wedges.

Makes about 8 servings.

Variation
Pine Nut and Onion Tartare: Arrange the *kibbeh nayee* into 12 small round or oval patties. Press the edges with the tines of a fork. Top each with minced onion and toasted whole pine nuts. Drizzle with olive oil and garnish with chopped parsley. Offer crushed red pepper flakes for those who like it hot!

BAKED MEAT DIAMONDS
(Kibbeh Sinayee)

Kibbeh Sinayee means *Kibbeh* in a pan. Most Middle Easterners serve this traditional dish as an entrée. Here we suggest serving these diamond-shaped portions as an appetizer with pita wedges. They're sure to bring raves.

1 recipe Kibbeh (Middle Eastern Meatballs), page 51, prepared through step 3
2 tablespoons butter
1 medium onion, chopped
½ pound ground lamb
2 tablespoons pine nuts
½ teaspoon ground cinnamon
Salt and pepper, to taste
2 tablespoons Yogurt Cheese, page 33
⅓ cup clarified butter, melted (see note)

Whole-Wheat Honey Pitas, page 23, cut into wedges

1.   Refrigerate the *kibbeh*, covered, until ready to bake.

2.   To prepare the filling, melt the butter in a medium skillet. Add the onions and sauté over medium heat, until tender and transparent, about 5 minutes. Add the lamb, pine nuts, cinnamon, salt, and pepper. Cook, stirring constantly, until the meat is

crumbled and lightly browned, about 15 minutes.

3. Remove from the heat and stir in the yogurt cheese. Blend until well mixed. Cool in the skillet at room temperature.

4. Preheat the oven to 400°F.

5. Thoroughly grease the bottom and sides of an 8- or 9-inch square or round baking pan with 2 tablespoons of the melted clarified butter. Prepare a bowl of ice and water. Place half the *kibbeh* in the pan, spreading it evenly. Pat the surface smooth. Dip your hands in the ice and water to prevent the *kibbeh* from sticking to your fingers. Cover with the filling, spreading it evenly.

Spread the remaining *kibbeh* to cover the filling and pat the surface smooth.

6. With your forefinger, press a hole in the center and each corner of the pan to help disperse the butter during baking. With a sharp knife, score into diamond shapes. Score completely through the mixture diagonally at 1½-inch intervals across the pan. Diagonally crisscross scores over these to make the diamond shapes. See illustration. Drizzle the *kibbeh* with the remaining clarified butter.

7. Bake until browned and firm, 30 to 45 minutes. Remove and let cool to lukewarm.

Cut an X through the center of the meat.

Continue making cuts across the pan. Diagonally crisscross cuts over the first set to make the diamonds.

8. Cut out the diamond shapes. Remove from the pan with a long thin spatula. Serve warm with whole-wheat honey pita wedges.

Makes about 40 diamonds.

Note: To clarify butter, melt unsalted or salted butter in a heavy saucepan over very low heat. Simmer slowly to allow the dairy solids and salt, if any, to rise to the top. Skim constantly until all the dairy solids have been removed and the butter is clear. (Save the skimmings to season freshly cooked vegetables). I usually clarify about 4 to 5 pounds of butter at a time. It will keep refrigerated indefinitely, although it need not be refrigerated for short-term use. Once heated, butter develops its own built-in preservative.

Variation
Stuffed Kibbeh (Kibbeh Ahkras): Instead of baking the *kibbeh* with the filling and cutting into diamond shapes, make stuffed meat balls. *Ahkras* means oval in Arabic and the children in Middle Eastern homes often refer to these stuffed delicacies as footballs since the most skillful cooks taper the ends to resemble a football!

1. Divide the *kibbeh* into 18 to 20 balls.

2. Prepare the filling for Baked Meat Diamonds, through step 3.

3. Dipping your hands in a bowl of ice and water to prevent sticking, press a cavity about 1½ to 2-inches deep into each ball. Divide the filling evenly among the balls and place 1 portion into each cavity.

4. Pinch the openings closed and shape into balls, cakes, or football-shaped ovals, about 2 to 2½-inches in diameter.

5. Pour the oil to a depth of ½ inch in a large skillet and heat until hot but not smoking. Working in batches, add the balls in a single layer and cook over medium-high heat, turning often until evenly browned and cooked through, 5 to 8 minutes. Add more oil to the skillet, if necessary, to cook the remaining balls. Drain on paper towels.

6. Serve them as appetizers accompanied by pita wedges and yogurt-garlic sauce, page 52.

Makes 18 to 20 stuffed balls.

While *frying* is a popular method of cookery in the Middle East for meatballs or patties and vegetable slices, *broiling* is an acceptable and preferable substitute for dieters. Brush the patties or vegetables with a little oil before broiling.

MEDITERRANEAN SHRIMP PATE
(Kibbeh Samak)

This traditional hot-weather dish from the Eastern shores of the Mediterranean is a fragrant blend of shrimp, bulgur, coriander, and sweet onion pressed atop a layer of thinly sliced onion and pine nuts, cut into diamond shapes, then baked to a turn. Similar in character to a pâté, it is served at room temperature as an appetizer, a main dish, or as a pita sandwich, topped with Carrot, Orange and Radish Salad, page 94. Make this dish a day in advance as it improves in flavor when refrigerated overnight.

3¼ pounds medium shrimp, shelled and deveined (2½ pounds shelled shrimp)
4 teaspoons salt
Dash of cinnamon
2 cups fine-grade bulgur
3 large onions
2 tablespoons ground coriander
1 tablespoon grated orange rind
½ teaspoon pepper
1¼ cups vegetable oil
½ cup pine nuts
Shredded romaine lettuce leaves
Lemon wedges (garnish)
Basic Pitas, page 21, cut into wedges

1. To prepare the shrimp, place them in a large bowl and sprinkle lightly with ½ teaspoon salt and the cinnamon. Toss to coat evenly. Refrigerate, covered, to chill for several hours or overnight. Drain.

2. To prepare the bulgur, rinse the grains and place them in a medium bowl. Cover with cool water and let soak until tender to the bite, 20 to 30 minutes. Drain thoroughly and squeeze out any excess water. Fluff to separate the grains. Refrigerate, covered, until ready to use.

3. To prepare the sliced onions, peel two of the onions, cut them in half lengthwise, then slice them very thin. Place them in a large bowl. Sprinkle lightly with ½ teaspoon salt and toss to coat evenly. Let stand until they are limp and moist. Squeeze out all the water and set aside.

4. Peel the remaining onion and cut it into quarters.

5. Place half of the shrimp and two onion quarters in a food processor fitted with the metal blade. Process carefully to a medium texture (or grind in a food grinder using the fine cutting wheel). Transfer to a mixing bowl. Repeat with the remaining half of the shrimp and onion quarters.

6. Prepare a bowl of ice and water. Add the bulgur to the shrimp-onion mixture and knead thoroughly until well blended, keeping your hands cool by dipping them in the bowl of ice and water. Add the coriander, orange rind, the remaining salt, and the pepper. Mix well.

7. Working in two batches, place half the shrimp-bulgur mixture in the food processor and process carefully to a fine texture (or grind the mixture in a food grinder as above). Be careful not to overprocess or the pâté mixture will be pasty. Repeat with the remaining mixture. Combine the 2 batches.

8. Preheat the oven to 450°F.

9. To bake and serve the pâté, pour ¼ cup of the oil into a 10 x 15-inch baking pan (see note). Coat the bottom and sides thoroughly. Layer the sliced onions and the pine nuts evenly over the bottom of the pan.

10. Scoop up a handful of the shrimp-bulgur mixture and flatten it between the palms of both hands. Beginning at one corner of the pan, place the mixture carefully over the onions and pine nuts. Continue with the remaining shrimp-bulgur mixture, until the entire layer of onions and nuts is covered to a depth of ½ to ¾-inch. Dipping your hands in ice water, pat the surface and edges smooth.

11. With your forefinger, press a hole in the center and at each corner of the pan to help disperse the oil during baking. With a sharp knife, score the pâté into diamond shapes. Score completely through the pâté diagonally at 1½-inch intervals across the pan. Diagonally crisscross scores over these to make the diamond shapes. See illustration on page 55. Carefully coat the surface with the remaining oil.

12. Bake until the loaf is golden brown and firm and the oil is bubbling, about 50 to 60 minutes. Remove from the oven and drain the remaining oil from the pan. To retain the moisture, cover the pan with a baking sheet. Let the covered pâté cool completely in the pan.

13. Place the lettuce on a serving platter. Cut out the diamond shapes and remove the pâté from the pan with a long thin spatula; be careful to get all the onions and pine nuts with each piece. Arrange the pâté nut-side-up on the lettuce. Garnish with the lemon wedges. Pass basic pita wedges as an accompaniment.

Makes 10 to 12 servings.

Note: Since the kibbeh should be between ½ to ¾-inch thick when baked, using the right size pan is important. If you vary the pan size, make sure your pâté doesn't get too thick or thin.

SPINACH AND RAISIN TRIANGLES
(Fatayer Sabanich)

For a delicious change of pace, try these tart spinach triangles made with Basic Pita dough. It is important to sprinkle the fresh spinach with salt as the recipe directs. This allows it to wilt so you can squeeze out the water before you prepare the filling. Otherwise, the water will seep out during the baking, making the triangles soggy. This recipe takes a little time, but the results make the effort well worth it. Served warm or cold, Spinach and Raisin Triangles make excellent appetizers and, because they carry well without refrigeration, also make great picnic fare.

2 pounds fresh spinach, stems trimmed, rinsed, coarsely chopped, and patted dry, or 3 packages (10 ounces each) frozen chopped spinach, thawed, squeezed dry, and fluffed to separate
Salt
½ to ¾ cup raisins
1¼ cup fresh lemon juice
1 large onion, finely chopped
½ cup olive oil
¾ cup coarsely chopped walnuts
Freshly ground black pepper, to taste
1 recipe Basic Pita dough, page 21, prepared through step 2
½ cup clarified butter, melted, page 56

1. Place the spinach in a colander. (If you are using fresh spinach, sprinkle lightly with salt and let stand until wilted. Squeeze to remove as much liquid as possible.)

2. Soak the raisins in boiling water until they are plumped, about 5 to 10 minutes. Drain thoroughly and dry with paper towels.

3. Combine the spinach and raisins with the lemon juice, onion, olive oil, walnuts, and pepper. Taste to correct seasonings. Set aside.

4. Divide the pita dough into 48 portions and shape each portion into a smooth ball. Place the balls on a floured work surface, and cover with slightly damp towels to keep the surface of the dough damp and moist. Let rest 30 to 45 minutes in a warm draft-free place.

5. Place 1 rack near the bottom third of the oven and another one just above it. Preheat the oven to 425°F. Lightly grease 2 baking sheets.

6. Working in 2 batches of 24 pies at a time, gently press each ball flat with your fingers, keeping it well rounded. Flour a work surface and rolling pin. Roll each round of dough into a 3½-inch circle.

7. Divide the spinach mixture equally into 48 portions, about 1½ to 2 rounded tablespoons each, and place 1 portion in the center of each circle being careful to drain off most of the liquid. Pick up the edges and pinch 3 sides of each circle firmly together to form a triangle, sealing the top of the triangle completely. Make certain that all the sides are well sealed to keep the juices from oozing out during baking. See illustration, page 67.

8. Arrange 12 triangles on each of the 2 greased baking sheets. Lightly brush with clarified butter.

9. Bake 2 sheets at a time, placing 1 sheet on each pre-positioned oven rack staggering 1 on the right and 1 on the left. Reverse the sheets from the top to bottom oven racks halfway through baking for even heat distribution. Bake until lightly browned, 15 to 20 minutes.

10. Repeat the process with the remaining 24 rounds of dough and the spinach mixture while the first batch bakes.

11. Remove the baked triangles from the oven and brush again with the clarified butter. Serve immediately or cool on wire racks and refrigerate, covered, for up to 1 week

or freeze for up to 3 months. To serve, thaw in the refrigerator overnight. Serve at room temperature or reheat in a preheated 325°F oven for 10 to 15 minutes.

12. Bake the remaining 24 triangles following the same method.

Makes 4 dozen triangles.

Anything-Goes Holiday Buffet

Taramosalata with Buttered
  Pita Toast
Spinach and Feta Triangles
Homemade Roasted Peppers
Mediterranean Shrimp Pâté
  with Basic Pita wedges
Chef's Couscous Salad with
  Wheat-Germ Honey Pitas
Curried Spinach, Walnut, and
  Orange Salad
Pita Cheese Crêpes with Rose
  Water Syrup
Orangeade with orange-
  blossom water
Coffee or Tea

SPINACH AND FETA TRIANGLES

This traditional fill-ing for a Greek *Spanakopita* stars here as a filling for a pita dough triangle, instead of the very rich butter-laced phyllo dough. Made without butter and eggs, this version is a healthy alternative to a popular appetizer—and tasty, too!

2 pounds fresh spinach, stems trimmed, rinsed, coarsely chopped, and patted dry, or 3 packages (10 ounces each) frozen chopped spinach, thawed, squeezed dry, and fluffed to separate
Salt
½ cup olive oil
2 medium onions, finely chopped
Freshly ground black pepper, to taste
¼ teaspoon nutmeg, or to taste
½ cup snipped fresh dill or 2 tablespoons dried dill
1¼ cups ricotta cheese
1 cup finely crumbled feta cheese
1 recipe Basic Pita dough, page 21, prepared through step 2

1. Place the spinach in a colander. (If you are using fresh spinach, sprinkle lightly with salt and let stand until wilted. Squeeze to re-move as much liquid as possible.)

2. Heat ¼ cup of the olive oil in a large skillet. Add the onions and sauté over medium heat until trans-lucent, about 5 minutes. Add the spinach and cook over low heat, stirring constantly, until the mix-ture is cooked through, about 10 minutes. Add the pepper and nut-meg. Cool to room temperature.

3. Blend in the dill and ricotta and feta cheeses. Taste to correct sea-sonings. Refrigerate, covered, until ready to fill the triangles.

4. Divide the pita dough into 48 portions and shape each portion into a smooth ball. Place the balls on a floured work surface and cover with slightly damp towels to keep the surface of the dough damp and moist. Let rest 30 to 45 minutes in a warm draft-free place.

5. Place 1 rack near the bottom third of the oven and another one just above it. Preheat the oven to 425°F. Lightly grease 2 baking sheets.

6. Working in 2 batches of 24 pies at a time, gently press each ball flat with your fingers, keeping it well rounded. Flour a work surface and rolling pin. Roll each round of dough into a 3½-inch circle.

7. Divide the spinach mixture equally into 48 portions, about 1 to 2 rounded tablespoons each, and place 1 portion in the center of each circle. Pick up the edges and pinch 3 sides of each circle firmly together to form a triangle, sealing the top of the triangle completely. Make certain that all the sides are well sealed to keep the juices from oozing out during baking. See illustration, page 67.

8. Arrange the 12 triangles on each of the 2 greased baking sheets. Lightly brush with olive oil.

9. Bake 2 sheets at a time, placing 1 sheet on each pre-positioned oven rack staggering 1 on the right and 1 on the left. Reverse the sheets from the top to bottom oven racks halfway through baking for even heat distribution. Bake until lightly browned, 15 to 20 minutes.

10. Repeat the process with the remaining 24 rounds of dough and the spinach-cheese mixture while the first batch bakes.

11. Remove the baked triangles from the oven and brush again with oil. Serve immediately or cool on wire racks and refrigerate, covered, for up to 3 days or freeze for up to 3 months. To serve, thaw in the refrigerator overnight. Reheat in a preheated 325°F oven for 10 to 15 minutes before serving.

12. Bake the remaining 24 triangles following the same method.

Makes 4 dozen appetizer pies.

Spinach and Cheese Omelet

This spinach and onion blend, seasoned with ricotta and feta cheeses, also makes an excellent filling for a breakfast or luncheon omelet. Serve it topped with a dollop of yogurt.

FLUTED PITA MEAT PIES

The aroma wafting its way from the oven as these savory pies bake to a turn is enough to tempt even the most disciplined dieter! Circles of Basic Pita dough are rolled then topped with a spicy blend of ground lamb, tomatoes, parsley, and cayenne, and closed to a fluted perfection. Serve them piping hot from the oven as appetizers with Taratour (Sesame and Garlic Sauce). While you're at it, freeze a batch for make-ahead convenience! What a treat unexpected guests have in store! Vary these fluted dainties the next time around by using the ground lamb, cinnamon, and yogurt filling in Pita Pyramids, page 66.

2 pounds ground lean lamb or beef
1 large onion, finely chopped
3 large fresh tomatoes, peeled, seeded, chopped, and squeezed to remove as much liquid as possible; or 1 can (28 ounces) whole tomatoes, drained, squeezed and mashed
½ cup tomato sauce
1 tablespoon finely chopped fresh parsley
Salt and freshly ground black pepper, to taste
Dash of cayenne
1 recipe Basic Pita dough, page 21, prepared through step 2
½ cup clarified butter, melted, page 56
Taratour (sesame and garlic sauce; recipe follows)

1. Combine the meat, onion, tomatoes, tomato sauce, parsley, salt, pepper, and cayenne in a medium bowl. Mix thoroughly. Refrigerate, covered, to chill.

2. Divide the pita dough into 48 portions. Shape each portion into a smooth ball. Place on a floured work surface and cover with slightly damp towels to keep the surface of the dough supple and moist. Let rest 30 to 45 minutes in a warm, draft-free place.

3. Place 1 rack near the bottom third of the oven and another one just above it. Preheat the oven to 425°F. Lightly grease 2 baking sheets.

Center filling on dough.

Bring up the dough edge, and use your fingers, to make tucks around the pie.

4. Working in 2 batches of 24 pies at a time, gently press each ball flat with your fingers, keeping it well rounded. Flour a work surface and rolling pin. Roll each round of dough into a 3½-inch circle.

5. Divide the meat mixture equally into 48 portions, about 1 rounded tablespoon each, and place 1 portion in the center of each circle. Flute the sides by bringing folds to within 1 inch of the center. See illustration on page 63. Press the fluted edges down firmly.

6. Arrange 12 pies on each of the 2 greased baking sheets. Lightly brush with clarified butter.

7. Bake 2 sheets at a time, placing 1 sheet on each pre-positioned oven rack staggering 1 on the right and 1 on the left. Reverse the sheets from the top to bottom racks halfway through baking for even heat distribution. Bake until lightly browned, 20 to 25 minutes.

8. Repeat the process with the remaining 24 rounds of dough and the meat mixture while the first batch bakes.

9. Remove the baked pies from the oven and brush again with clarified butter. Serve immediately or cool on wire racks and refrigerate, covered, for up to 3 days or freeze for up to 3 months. To serve, thaw in the refrigerator overnight. Reheat in a preheated 325°F oven for 10 to 15 minutes before serving.

10. Bake the remaining 24 pies following the same method.

Makes 4 dozen appetizer pies.

LEMONADE WITH ORANGE-BLOSSOM WATER

As a child, I recall my mother served this tall cool glass of "heaven" to her church circle group. When I was old enough to start cooking, I found out its secret ingredient was orange-blossom water!

⅓ cup fresh lemon juice
2 cups ice water
½ to 1 teaspoon orange-blossom water, to taste

Sugar, to taste
Ice
Lemon slices (garnish)
Fresh mint sprigs (garnish)

Combine the lemon juice, ice water, orange-blossom water, and sugar in a pitcher. Blend well. Pour into ice-filled glasses. Garnish with lemon slices and mint sprigs.

Makes 2 to 3 servings.

TARATOUR
(Sesame and Garlic Sauce)

Throughout the Middle East, this classic sauce appears in many forms and with numerous subtle variations in seasonings. Basically a mixture of Tahini (sesame seed paste), garlic, lemon juice, salt, and pepper, it is used as a sauce for steamed or fried vegetables, a dip for crudités or pita crisps, and thinned, as a salad dressing or topping for pita sandwiches.

1 cup Tahini (sesame seed paste), page 41
2 cloves garlic, crushed
⅓ cup fresh lemon juice
Salt and freshly ground black pepper, to taste
¼ to ½ cup water
Chopped fresh parsley (garnish)

1. Combine the tahini, garlic, lemon juice, salt, and pepper in a bowl or blender. Mix or blend until smooth.

2. Gradually add the water until the sauce reaches the desired consistency. The dip should be thicker than a dressing or sauce. Taste to correct seasonings. Pour into a medium bowl. Garnish with the chopped parsley.

Makes about 2 cups.

A Middle Eastern Sunday Supper

Hot Hummus and Feta Cheese with Sesame Pita Crisps/ Whole-Wheat Honey Pita wedges
Pita Pyramids
Middle-Eastern Meatballs with Basic Pitas
Cucumber and Yogurt Salad
Glazed Pita Puffs
Spiced Turkish Coffee

PITA PYRAMIDS
(Fatayer)

Every country has its own version of meat pies or turnovers. *Fatayer* belongs to the Arab world. They may be round and fluted, rolled, turned over, or, as we've done here, shaped into a pyramid or triangle. Pita dough is a chewy natural wrap for these tart and tangy fillings of ground lamb or beef, cinnamon, yogurt, and pine nuts. Make the pies soft and buttery by brushing them with clarified butter as they come piping hot from the oven.

2 pounds ground lean lamb or beef
1 large onion, finely chopped
½ cup plain yogurt, preferably homemade, page 32
¼ teaspoon ground cinnamon
Salt and freshly ground black pepper, to taste
½ cup pine nuts
1 recipe Basic Pita dough, page 21, prepared through step 2
½ cup clarified butter, melted, page 56
Yogurt-Garlic Sauce, page 52

1. Combine the meat, onion, yogurt, cinnamon, salt, pepper, and pine nuts in a medium bowl. Mix thoroughly. Refrigerate, covered, to chill.

2. Divide the pita dough into 48 portions. Shape each portion into a smooth ball. Place on a floured work surface and cover with slightly damp towels to keep the surface of the dough supple and moist. Let rest 30 to 45 minutes in a warm draft-free place.

3. Place 1 rack near the bottom third of the oven and another one just above it. Preheat the oven to 425°F. Lightly grease 2 baking sheets.

4. Working in 2 batches of 24 pies at a time, gently press each ball flat with your fingers, keeping it well rounded. Flour a work surface and a rolling pin. Roll each round of dough into a 3½-inch circle.

5. Divide the meat mixture equally into 48 portions, about 1 rounded tablespoon each, and place 1 portion in the center of each circle. Pick up the edges and pinch 3 sides of each circle firmly together, leaving a small opening in the center, to form a triangle. See illustration on opposite page.

6. Arrange 12 pies on each of the 2 greased baking sheets. Lightly brush with clarified butter. Press the tops slightly to close the edges securely.

7. Bake 2 sheets at a time, placing 1 sheet on each pre-positioned oven rack staggering 1 on the right and 1 on the left. Reverse the sheets from the top to bottom racks halfway through baking for even heat distribution. Bake until lightly browned, 20 to 25 minutes.

8. Repeat the process with the remaining 24 rounds of dough and the meat mixture while the first batch bakes.

9. Remove the baked pies from the oven and brush again with clarified butter. Serve immediately or cool on wire racks and refrigerate, covered, for up to 3 days or freeze for up to 3 months. To serve, thaw in the refrigerator overnight. Reheat in a preheated 325°F oven until warmed through, about 15 minutes.

10. Bake the remaining 24 pies, following the same method.

Makes 4 dozen appetizer pies.

Tip

For dinner-size servings, divide the dough into 24 equal portions and roll each into a 5- or 6-inch circle. Divide the filling evenly among the 24 pies and close. Makes 2 dozen large pies.

Center filling on dough.

Pinch up two-thirds of the dough edge. Then bring up the third.

For pyramids leave a small opening at the top. For triangles, seal the seams tightly.

SQUASH PATTIES WITH YOGURT-GARLIC SAUCE

These unusual patties, first cousins to potato pancakes, are especially good topped with a dollop of Yogurt-Garlic Sauce.

2 cups shredded zucchini or yellow squash
Salt
2 eggs, beaten
1 small onion, minced
Freshly ground black pepper, to taste
About ½ cup unbleached all-purpose flour
Vegetable oil, for frying
Yogurt-Garlic Sauce, page 52
Sesame Pitas, page 22, cut into wedges

1. Place the squash in a colander set over a medium bowl. Sprinkle lightly with salt and toss to mix. Set aside for 30 minutes. Squeeze out the water. Pat the squash dry on paper towels.

2. Return the squash to the bowl and add the eggs, onion, and pepper, and stir to blend. Gradually add up to ½ cup flour, stirring, to bind the mixture. Divide into 12 patties.

3. Pour the oil to a depth of ¼ inch in a heavy skillet and heat until hot but not smoking. Working in batches, add the patties and fry over medium heat, turning once, until golden-brown, about 2 minutes. Remove with a slotted spoon and drain on paper towels. Add more oil, if necessary, for subsequent batches.

4. Serve the squash patties drizzled with the yogurt-garlic sauce and surrounded by freshly made sesame pita wedges.

Makes 12 patties.

FRIED EGGPLANT AND SQUASH WITH TARATOUR

Easy to make and delectable, these are a great addition to the *meze* spread.

1 small eggplant, peeled, halved lengthwise, and cut into ¼-inch slices

3 medium zucchini or yellow squash (about 2 inches in diameter), peeled, halved lengthwise, and cut into ¼-inch slices

Salt

Vegetable oil, for frying

Taratour (sesame and garlic sauce), page 65

Basic Pitas, page 21, cut into wedges

1. Lightly salt both sides of the eggplant and squash slices. Layer them on paper towels and cover the top with another layer of paper towels. Set aside for 1 hour to drain off excess moisture. Pat dry with fresh paper towels.

2. Pour the oil to a depth of ¼ inch in a heavy skillet and heat until hot but not smoking. Working in batches, add the eggplant and squash and fry over medium heat until golden-brown, 2 to 3 minutes. Remove with a slotted spoon and drain on paper towels. Add more oil, if necessary, for subsequent batches.

3. Arrange the eggplant and squash slices on a serving platter and lace with taratour (sesame and garlic sauce). Surround with pita wedges and offer a bowl of additional sauce for those who may want more.

Makes 6 to 8 servings.

Tip

Both squash patties and fried eggplant and squash slices also make wonderful pita sandwiches when laced with yogurt-garlic sauce or taratour and topped with shredded romaine lettuce.

HOT BON CHAMPIGNON BRIE ON DUXELLES

Mushroom duxelles, that dry, delicious mushroom flavoring, used generously by French chefs for many kinds of stuffings and sauces, makes a wonderful base for Bon Champignon cheese-stuffed pitas. This is a great way to use up leftover pieces of plain brie, even through I've suggested using the mushroom brie as a starter. I like the "double-champignon" flavor. And if you don't make the duxelles, mushroom brie used alone is super!

*Medium Basic Pitas, page 21, split
   into rounds*
1 recipe Duxelles (recipe follows)
*Mushroom Brie (Bon Champignon
   or Mushroom Saga), sliced into ⅛
   to ¼-inch wedges*

1.   Preheat the broiler.

2.   Lightly spread the bottom rounds of the pitas with a layer of duxelles. Top with slices of mushroom brie and place on a baking sheet. Broil until hot and bubbly, about 5 minutes.

3.   Place the pita top on the hot brie and bake in a preheated 325°F oven until the top is warm, 1 to 2 minutes.

4.   Slice into wedges with a serrated knife and serve immediately.

Duxelles

*1 pound fresh mushrooms, wiped
   clean with damp paper towels
   and finely minced*
¼ cup butter
2 tablespoons vegetable oil
¼ cup minced shallots (4 medium)
*Salt and freshly ground black
   pepper, to taste*
½ cup dry white wine

1.   Working in batches over a bowl, squeeze small scoops of the mushrooms into tight balls in a paper towel to remove as much liquid as possible; reserve the liquid.

2.   Melt the butter in the oil in a large skillet. Add the mushrooms and shallots and sauté over medium heat, stirring frequently, until they begin to dry out and brown, about 10 to 12 minutes. Season with salt and pepper to taste.

3.   Add the wine and reserved mushroom liquid and continue to cook over medium-high heat until all the liquid has evaporated. Cool and use as desired. To store, refrigerate, covered, for up to 1 week or freeze for up to 3 months.

Makes about 1½ to 2 cups duxelles.

GINGERED FIG MONTRACHET

Since early times, figs have been revered by the Hebrews as a reflection of peace and plenty. Today both green and purple figs are plumper and sweeter than ever, thanks to modern-day cultivation. To prove it, we've combined fresh purple figs and minced ginger with softened Montrachet to make a delightful goat cheese spread. Offer crunchy pita crisps and serve a dry white wine or a spiced herbal tea to accompany this elegant offering.

1 log (12 ounces) Montrachet
2 to 4 tablespoons half-and-half
3 to 4 ripe purple figs, finely chopped
1 teaspoon finely minced fresh ginger
1 tablespoon fresh lemon juice, to taste
Freshly ground black pepper, to taste
Sweet Sesame Pita Crisps, page 28

1. Break up the log of Montrachet and place in a blender or food processor fitted with the metal blade. With the machine running, add the half-and-half in a thin steady stream. Process until the mixture is creamy and spreadable.

2. Transfer the cheese mixture to a medium bowl and add the remaining ingredients except the pita crisps. Mix gently until well blended. Refrigerate, covered, to chill.

3. Transfer the spread to a serving bowl. Offer with sweet sesame pita crisps.

Makes about 2 cups.

Sunny Sunday Brunch

Orange-blossom Screwdrivers
Fresh melon slices with pomegranate garnish
Hot Bon Champignon Brie on Duxelles in a Pita
Classic Parsley and Onion Omelet Wedges in buttered Basic Pita wedges
Spinach and Feta Triangles
Coriander and Lamb Sausage Patties wrapped in Griddle-Baked Pitas
Spiced Glazed Figs with Hazelnuts and Sweetened Sesame Pitas
Coffee or Tea

FRIED LEMON-LACED CHEESE

A lacing of lemon juice gives a classic fried-cheese appetizer an entirely new and lively personality. To give the cheese cubes more body when they are fried, chill them, uncovered, in the refrigerator for several hours. They are particularly tasty when wrapped in Griddle-Baked Pitas and served with apple wedges, grapes, or fresh white figs, and a bottle of your favorite white wine.

1 pound hard, dry cheese (Kasseri, or Fontina)
1 large clove garlic, cut in half
½ cup unbleached all-purpose flour
½ teaspoon crumbled dried thyme
¼ cup vegetable oil
2 tablespoons fresh lemon juice
Lemon wedges (garnish)
Griddle-Baked Pitas, page 31

1. Rub the cheese with the cut garlic, then cut into 1½-inch cubes. Refrigerate to chill.

2. Combine the flour and thyme in a small bowl. Blend thoroughly. Dredge the cheese cubes in the flour.

3. Heat the oil in a large skillet until it is hot but not smoking. Add the coated cubes, and fry, over medium-high heat, turning frequently, until brown on all sides but not melted, about 1½ to 2 minutes.

4. Place the cheese on a warm serving platter and lace with the lemon juice. Garnish with lemon wedges and serve immediately. Surround with griddle-baked pitas which guests may use to wrap around these delicate morsels.

Makes 6 to 8 servings.

BASIL FONDUE PIEDMONTESE

This is a Middle Eastern version of the famous Fondue Piedmontese. Instead of surrounding the cheese fondue with sautéed slices of Italian bread, I've used Pita Crisps. And instead of garnishing the fondue with truffles, I've opted for the less expensive but delicious black Greek olives.

¼ pound (about 1 cup) Fontina cheese, diced, or ¼ pound mozzarella, diced
¼ cup grated Swiss cheese
1 tablespoon potato starch
¾ cup milk
1 egg yolk
1 tablespoon finely chopped fresh basil
1 tablespoon sliced black Greek olives (garnish)
Savory Pita Crisps, page 28

1. Put the diced and grated cheeses into the top of a double boiler.

2. Blend the potato starch with the milk and egg yolk. Add to the cheeses.

3. Add the basil and stir the cheese-milk mixture over simmering water until completely melted and smooth. Pour into a heated serving bowl or small chafing dish. Garnish with the olives and surround with a variety of savory pita crisps. Serve immediately.

Makes about 2 cups.

WALNUT-STUFFED GRAPE LEAVES

Vegetable and nut-stuffed grape leaves cooked in olive oil and lemon juice are a variation of meat-stuffed grape leaves adapted originally by families observing the meatless Lenten season. Today these tart yet sweetish delicacies are a popular appetizer accompanied by soft pita. Serve them at room temperature to bring out the flavors.

1 jar (1 pound) pickled grape leaves
    (50 to 60 leaves)
½ cup olive oil, plus oil for
    drizzling
1 large onion, finely chopped
1 cup long-grain rice
½ cup chopped walnuts
⅓ cup golden raisins
2 teaspoons chopped fresh dill
½ teaspoon ground cinnamon
Salt and freshly ground black
    pepper, to taste
½ cup fresh lemon juice
2 to 2½ cups boiling water
Lemon wedges
Whole-Wheat Honey Pitas, page 23,
    cut into wedges

1. Drain the grape leaves and soak them in cold water for about 30 minutes. Drain and rinse them again until all the salt is removed then squeeze them gently to remove excess moisture. Cut off the stems and set aside.

2. Heat ½ cup of olive oil in a large skillet. Add the onions and sauté over medium heat until soft and transparent, about 5 minutes. Add the rice and toss to coat with the oil. Add the walnuts, raisins, dill, cinnamon, salt, and pepper. Taste to correct seasonings. Remove from the heat and let cool.

3. Drizzle the bottom of a Dutch oven with olive oil and line it with a single layer of grape leaves.

4. To stuff the remaining leaves, place each leaf, vein-side up, on a plate or cutting board. Spoon about 1 tablespoon of the rice mixture in the center of each leaf. Tuck the bottom of the leaf over the filling, fold the sides over the center, and roll up into a tight, neat packet. Stack the stuffed grape leaves, folded-side down, in a single layer in the Dutch oven. Arrange a second layer at right angles to the first. See illustration.

5. Mix the lemon juice with at least 2 cups of boiling water and pour over the grape leaves. Invert a heat-proof plate over the layers to hold them in place during cooking. Add more boiling water (up to ½ cup), if necessary, to reach the top of the inverted plate. Cover and simmer over medium-low heat until the rice is tender to the bite, about 45 minutes. Drain the liquid and cool.

6. Serve at room temperature garnished with lemon wedges. Offer guests a basket of basic pita wedges to mop up the lemony liquid.

Makes about 50 to 60 stuffed grape leaves.

Variation *Tabbouleh-Stuffed Grape Leaves:* Stuff each grape leaf with 1 tablespoon of tabbouleh (page 98) and cook as above.

Fluffy Rice? Add Lemon!

For stuffed grape or cabbage leaves or any rice stuffing mixtures, add a tablespoon of fresh lemon juice to each cup of rice. This will ensure fluffy, tender, separate grains of rice every time.

Center filling on leaf.

Tuck the bottom of the leaf over filling.

Fold sides toward the center and continue rolling into a tight packet.

OLIVE PASTE TARTS WITH YOGURT CHEESE

Here toasted pita rounds are topped with Fresh Yogurt Cheese then spread with a tangy olive paste and sprinkled with dried mint. This olive paste is similar to a traditional French tapenade, minus the anchovies which seem to overpower the distinctive flavor of the capers. This makes an excellent appetizer or an unusual breakfast spread when served with pita toast.

1½ cups black Greek olives, pitted
2 tablespoons capers, drained
1 clove garlic, sliced
1 tablespoon fresh lemon juice
½ to 1 teaspoon Dijon-style mustard, to taste
Freshly ground black pepper, to taste
1 tablespoon white wine
¼ to ½ cup olive oil
Small Basic Pitas, page 21, split into rounds and toasted
Yogurt Cheese, page 33

1. Combine the olives, capers, garlic, lemon juice, mustard, pepper, and white wine in a blender or food processor fitted with the metal blade and process until smooth.

2. With the machine running, add enough oil in a thin, steady stream to make a thick, smooth, spreadable paste. Taste to correct seasonings. Refrigerate, covered, to chill.

3. Spread the cooled, toasted pita rounds with the yogurt cheese. Top with a thin layer of the olive paste and serve as an appetizer or a breakfast spread.

Makes about 1½ cups.

Music-In-The-Park Supper

Champagne
Olive-Paste Tarts with Basic Pitas
Chicken Salad Béarnaise with Whole-Wheat Sesame Pitas
Market Salad with Basil Torta Vinaigrette
Spiced Glazed Figs with Hazelnuts
Spiced Turkish Coffee

OPEN-FACED GOAT CHEESE PITA TARTS

These savory tarts are made from a hard goat cheese that has been marinated in a vegetable broth laced with Cognac, then blended until smooth. Serve them hot straight from the broiler. Any remaining spread makes a great dip served with Garlic Pita Crisps.

1½ cups water
½ cup chopped leeks, both white and green
½ cup minced fresh chives or 3 tablespoons dried chives
1 tablespoon minced shallot
1 small bay leaf
1½ tablespoons Cognac
¼ teaspoon crumbled dried thyme
1 teaspoon minced fresh tarragon
¾ pound hard goat cheese—such as Crottin de Chavignol
Small Basic Pitas, page 21, split into rounds and toasted

1. Twenty-four hours before serving, combine all the ingredients except for ½ teaspoon of the tarragon, the cheese, and the pita in a medium saucepan. Bring to a boil, then reduce the heat and simmer, covered, for 30 minutes. Cool the broth to lukewarm and strain. Put the cheese and vegetable broth in an earthenware crock or glass bowl. Cover and refrigerate for 24 hours.

2. Preheat the broiler.

3. Place the cheese and broth in a blender or food processor fitted with the metal blade and process until smooth. Add more water or additional cheese if necessary to achieve a spreadable paste.

4. Spread the toasted pita rounds with the goat-cheese mixture and top with the remaining tarragon. Broil until warm and bubbly. Serve immediately.

Makes about 2 cups goat-cheese spread.

FRESH PITA PIZZA

Make a super pizza out of the Basic Pita dough—it is quite like the dough used for pizzas. Try it with a variety of fresh vegetables layered atop mounds of string cheese which is similar to mozzarella. Or, use shredded mozzarella if you prefer. Whichever you choose, this pizza will star as an appetizer or weekend snack.

Basic Pizza

½ recipe Basic Pita dough, page 21, prepared through step 2
¼ cup olive oil
8 ounces string cheese or shredded mozzarella
Salt and freshly ground black pepper, to taste
Pizza toppings (see below)
¼ cup chopped fresh cilantro
2 tablespoons grated Parmesan

Pizza Toppings

Lightly fried eggplant slices
Lightly fried squash slices
Chopped fresh tomato
Sliced green or red bell pepper
Sliced and sautéed fresh mushrooms
Lamb, onion, and pine nut sauté (filling used for Stuffed Kibbeh, page 56)
Pitted and sliced black Greek olives

1. Divide the dough into 2 portions. Shape each portion into a smooth ball. Place on a floured work surface and cover with slightly damp towels. Let rest in a warm draft-free place, 30 to 45 minutes.

2. Place a rack in the lowest position in the oven. Preheat the oven to 450°F. Lightly grease two 10- or 12-inch pizza pans or baking sheets.

3. Preparing 1 pizza at a time, gently press each ball flat with your fingers, keeping it well rounded. Flour a work surface and rolling pin. Roll the round of dough into a 10- or 12-inch circle, pulling at the edges with your fingers and turning several times until you reach the desired size. Gently place the circle on a pizza pan or baking sheet. Pinch the edges up slightly to form a ridge. Drizzle the circle with 2 tablespoons of olive oil and spread it to the rim.

4. Cover the pizza with 4 ounces of string cheese pulled into thin shreds or shredded mozzarella. Add salt, pepper, and a combination of toppings. Sprinkle with 2 tablespoons of cilantro and 1 tablespoon of grated Parmesan.

5. Bake until the crust is golden brown, 15 to 20 minutes. Remove from the oven.

6. Repeat the process with the second pizza.

7. Cut into wedges with a pizza cutter and serve immediately.

Makes two 10- or 12-inch pizzas.

MARINATED ARTICHOKES WITH SALONIKA PEPPERS

For a unique and different appetizer, try this medley of artichokes, black Greek olives, and Salonika peppers. The lustiness of the olives and the peppery Salonika perfectly complement the delicate artichokes.

1 package (10-ounces) frozen artichoke hearts, cooked, and drained, or 1 can (1 pound) artichoke hearts, drained
½ to ¾ cup black Greek olives
12 small Salonika peppers
¼ cup olive oil
1 tablespoon red wine vinegar
2 tablespoons fresh lemon juice
2 scallions, finely chopped
Salt and freshly ground black pepper, to taste
Finely chopped fresh cilantro (garnish)
Wheat-Germ Honey Pitas, page 24, cut into wedges

1. Combine the artichoke hearts, olives, and peppers in a medium bowl.

2. Blend the olive oil, vinegar, lemon juice, scallions, salt, and pepper in a small bowl. Taste to correct seasonings. Add the dressing to the salad mixture and toss to coat. Refrigerate, covered, for at least 2 hours or overnight.

3. Drain and discard the dressing. Serve the salad on a platter. Garnish with the cilantro. Serve wheat-germ honey pita wedges on the side.

Makes 6 appetizer servings.

ANTIPASTO PITA

Fill a Whole-Wheat Honey Pita with Genoa salami, cervalat, or pepperoni. Top with Homemade Roasted Peppers, page 80, chickpeas, sliced tomatoes, sweet onions, and mozzarella. Drizzle a little marinade from the roasted peppers over everything and garnish with chopped fresh basil leaves and pitted black Greek olives.

HOMEMADE ROASTED PEPPERS

Fresh sweet red bell peppers, roasted and charred to a soft perfection, are ideal for spiking up many salad fillings to stuff in a pita. They are also super additions to a charcuterie board or a Pita Antipasto spread, page 79.

8 medium (about 2½ pounds) red
   bell peppers
⅓ cup olive oil
3 tablespoons red wine vinegar
½ cup chopped scallions
Salt and freshly ground black
   pepper, to taste
1 clove garlic, cut in half

1. Preheat the oven to 450°F.

2. Wash and drain the peppers and place on a baking sheet. Bake, turning them about every 5 minutes, until the skins are charred and blistered, about 20 to 25 minutes.

3. Immediately transfer the peppers to a brown paper bag (or a covered Dutch oven) and close tightly. Let stand until the peppers are cool and the skins have begun to separate from the meat, about 20 to 30 minutes.

4. Peel off the skins, using a knife if necessary. Seed the peppers and remove the membranes. Cut into bite-size pieces.

5. Blend the olive oil, vinegar, scallions, salt, pepper, and garlic in a large bowl. Taste to correct seasonings. Add the peppers and toss gently to coat. Cover and marinate, in the refrigerator, turning occasionally, for at least 3 hours.

6. Serve at room temperature as a condiment with pita sandwiches, charcuterie, or a pita antipasto spread. To store, refrigerate, covered, for up to 1 week.

Makes about 1 quart.

PIQUANT PICKLED TURNIPS
(Lif-fit)

Piquant pink pickled turnips, called *Lif-fit* in Arabic, are classic Middle Eastern condiments served before or during a meal and always accompanied by pita, of course. These appetizer pickles get their pretty color by the addition of beets and beet juice to the pickling solution. Every time I share this recipe with friends, it becomes a part of their permanent culinary repertoire. Remember, though, that it takes three days to pickle the turnips, so plan ahead.

2½ to 3 pounds medium white turnips
Salt
1 pound small whole beets, cooked, peeled, and juice reserved or 1 can (1 pound) small whole beets, drained and juice reserved
Black peppercorns
1½ cups lukewarm water
1½ cups white vinegar
2 teaspoons salt or to taste

1. Three days before serving, wash the unpeeled turnips and slice off the tops and bottoms. Remove any brown spots with a vegetable brush or scrape lightly with a dull knife. Cut into halves, if small, or in quarters if large and place in a large bowl. Lightly salt and set aside at room temperature for 6 to 8 hours, frequently draining off excess water.

2. Place the turnips in 2 sterilized 1-quart glass jars. Add at least 2 beets and several peppercorns in each jar.

3. Combine the water, vinegar, salt, and ½ cup reserved beet juice in a bowl. Pour over the turnips, leaving ½ inch of space at the top (if you fill the jars to the top, the liquid may leak as the turnips begin their fermentation).

4. Seal and set aside in a cool place for three days to expedite the pickling process before refrigerating. Turn the jars upside down occasionally so the color is dispersed throughout and the top turnips are evenly coated and exposed to the pickling solution. Refrigerate after the third day.

Makes 2 quarts.

Tip

Easy appetizers that complement pita include:
● Marinated Calamata and Alphonse olives
● Fresh dates stuffed with unsalted Yogurt Cheese
● Sliced tomatoes sprinkled with fresh cilantro or basil and freshly ground black pepper
● Cold shrimp or diced avocado marinated in olive oil, lemon juice, crushed garlic, salt, and freshly ground black pepper

MARINATED BLACK GREEK OLIVES

Olives are always a part of a Middle Eastern *meze* spread. The choices are many although we prefer either the Calamata or Alfonse varieties since they are especially assertive in flavor and appearance. They are sold in brine, by the pound or packed in containers, and while they may be eaten as purchased, it is a good idea to marinate them first to subdue their saltiness and soften the flavor.

Soak the olives in cold water then drain them, repeating this process several times over a period of 2 to 3 hours or overnight to remove the excess brine. Taste them to test the flavor. Place 1 quart of olives in a clean jar and drizzle 1 tablespoon of olive oil and 1 teaspoon of wine vinegar over the top. Cover and turn the jar upside down several times to coat the olives.

Refrigerate to help retain the flavor. Before serving, set them out at room temperature and repeat the upside-down blending once more to coat the olives. This small amount of marinade gives them just a hint of flavor and adds an appetizing shimmer. You may use more olive oil and vinegar, if desired, though we find this proportion above is just enough to season and coat the olives yet keep them firm.

CAULIFLOWER AND ONION PICKLES
(Quarnabeet Bi Busil)

These tart cauli-
flower and onion
pickles, called *Quarna-
beet Bi Busil* in Arabic,
are a popular pre-
dinner appetizer at a
Mediterranean meal.
I've broken from clas-
sic tradition to include
small white onions as a
crunchy teammate.
Usually served with an
assortment of other
condiments, these
pickles seem to be the
first to go! Chopped
and coated with a light
drizzle of Taratour
(sesame and garlic
sauce), they also make
a delightful topping for
a *Falafel* or *Kibbeh*
sandwich.

*1 medium (about 2½ pounds)
cauliflower separated into florets
and parboiled*
*½ pound small white onions, about
1 to 1½-inches in diameter,
parboiled*
*1 pound small whole beets, cooked,
peeled, and juice reserved or 1
can (1 pound) small whole beets,
drained and juice reserved*
Black peppercorns
1½ cups lukewarm water
1½ cups white vinegar
Salt, to taste

1. Three days before serving,
place the cauliflower and the onions
in 2 sterilized 1-quart glass jars. Add
at least 2 beets and several peppercorns in each jar.

2. Combine the water, vinegar,
salt, and ½ cup reserved beet juice
in a bowl. Pour over the cauliflower
and onions, leaving ½ inch of space
at the top (if you fill the jars to the
top, the liquid may leak as the cauliflower and onions begin their fermentation).

3. Seal and set aside in a cool place
for three days to expedite the pickling process before refrigerating.
Turn the jars upside down occasionally so the color is dispersed
throughout and the top pickles are
evenly coated and exposed to the
pickling solution. Refrigerate after
the third day.

Makes 2 quarts.

PITA CHARCUTERIE

On a warm summer's evening, offer friends a Pita Charcuterie. Set
out basketsful of soft fresh pitas, a tray of thinly sliced meats including fresh roast pork, smoked turkey, and rare roast beef, and a se-
lection of pâtés and sausages. Condiments, of course, should abound—
mild and spicy mustards, sweet and dill pickles, Marinated Black Greek
Olives, page 82, Homemade Roasted Peppers, page 80, and Piquant
Pickled Turnips, page 81.

PITA ALONGSIDES

Traditionally soups and salads are served as separate courses of an elaborate meal, but nowadays they can be a complete meal in themselves with lots of warm pitas for dunking and scooping.

The soups I have included are based on simple Middle Eastern peasant fare—yogurt, legumes, spinach, pasta, mint, lemon, garlic, and olive oil—all the foods that go so well with pita. There's even a soup that uses pita dough in the form of dumplings. Make these soups ahead to enhance their flavors and reduce last-minute work.

As for the salads, many will double as appetizers and as toppings for a pita-filled sandwich while others are meals in themselves or make great accompaniments to other dishes. Tomato and Onion Salad, for instance, is often served at the *meze* spread and *Kibbeh* (Middle-Eastern Meatballs) stuffed into pitas and topped with Cucumber and Yogurt Salad make very tasty sandwiches. *Tabbouleh* can be served alongside so many of the dishes, while Chef's Couscous Salad, chock full of greens, bulgur, and tender slices of roast lamb and chicken, satisfies the appetite of the heartiest eater so long as there are plenty of pitas to scoop it all up, of course.

SPINACH AND LENTIL SOUP
(Addas Bi Hamoud)

This hearty potage of lentils and spinach, called *Addas Bi Hamoud* in Arabic and translated to mean a sour lentil soup or lentils with lemon, is a favorite in Middle Eastern homes. And you can bet it is always served with baskets full of warm pita. Make a double batch of this pita companion and freeze one for a cold winter's day. Serve it with Pita Bread Salad, page 101, for a hearty meal.

1½ cups lentils
2½ quarts water
1 tablespoon salt
¼ cup olive oil
1 large onion, chopped
1 clove garlic, crushed
2 medium potatoes, scrubbed, and diced with the skins left on (about 1½ cups)
10 ounces fresh spinach, rinsed, patted dry, stems trimmed, and leaves torn into bite-size pieces or 1 package (10 ounces) frozen leaf spinach
¼ cup fresh lemon juice, or to taste
1 teaspoon ground coriander
Freshly ground black pepper, to taste
Whole-Wheat Sesame Pitas, page 24, cut into wedges

1. Wash and drain the lentils. Put them in a large kettle and add the water. Bring to a boil and add the salt. Reduce the heat and simmer, covered, until the lentils are almost tender, 45 minutes to 1 hour.

2. Heat the oil in a large skillet. Add the onion and garlic and sauté over medium heat until soft and translucent, about 5 minutes.

3. Add the onion mixture to the lentils. Add the potatoes, spinach, 1 tablespoon lemon juice, coriander, and pepper. If you are using frozen spinach, drop the frozen block into the hot lentil mixture and break up with a fork as it cooks. Stir thoroughly. Simmer covered, until the potatoes are tender, about 15 to 20 minutes. If the soup seems too thick, add a little boiling water to thin the mixture.

4. Just before serving, add the remaining lemon juice. Taste to correct seasonings. Serve accompanied with wedges of whole-wheat sesame pita.

Makes 8 servings.

Tailgater Pita Party

Spinach and Lentil Soup with
    Whole-Wheat Sesame Pitas
Broiled Kefta Kebabs in
    Sesame Pitas
Spicy Bulgur Salad
Feta Cheese and Cucumber
    Salad
Glazed Pita Puffs
Hearty Burgundy
Lots of Hot Coffee

NOODLES AND LENTIL HOT POT
(Rishta)

Called *Rishta* in Arabic, this rich peasant soup is a relative to the lemony Spinach and Lentil Soup and it, too, calls for stacks of warm pita for dunking. Noodles are the classic ingredient, but you might like to substitute new potatoes and even add other favorite vegetables such as carrots or rutabagas. Serve it alongside a dish of Minted Cabbage Salad.

2 cups lentils
2 quarts water
1 tablespoon salt
⅓ cup olive oil
2 large onions, chopped
3 cloves garlic, finely chopped
1½ cups medium egg noodles
Freshly ground black pepper, to taste
Wheat-germ Honey Pitas, page 24, cut into wedges

1. Wash and drain the lentils. Put them in a large kettle and add the water. Bring to a boil and add the salt. Reduce the heat and simmer, covered, until the lentils are almost tender, 45 minutes to 1 hour.

2. Heat the oil in a large skillet. Add the onions and garlic, and sauté over medium heat until soft and translucent, about 5 minutes.

3. Add the onion mixture to the lentils. Add the noodles and pepper. Stir thoroughly. Simmer, covered, until the noodles are tender, about 20 to 25 minutes. If the soup seems too thick, add a little boiling water to thin the mixture. Taste to correct seasonings.

4. Serve accompanied with wedges of wheat-germ honey pita.

Makes 8 servings.

Vegetarian Supper

Squash Patties with Yogurt-Garlic Sauce
Noodles and Lentil Hot Pot with Wheat-Germ Honey Pitas
Falafel topped with Chopped Vegetable Salad in Basic Pitas
Fresh pears and string cheese with Sweet Sesame Pita Crisps
Cardamom Coffee

LITTLE PITA DUMPLINGS IN YOGURT SOUP
(Shish Barak Bi Laban)

This refreshingly delightful hot yogurt soup, dressed with garlic, melted butter, and fresh mint, shows off the tastiest little lamb and pine nut dumplings you've ever eaten. And conveniently, the dumplings are made with the same dough used to make Griddle-Baked Pita. With the dumpling-laden bowl of hot soup, chances are you won't need any bread, but I'll bet you can't resist a pita for dunking. Serve this accompanied by a crisp Classic Mediterranean Salad, page 94, and you've a memorable meal!

Pita Dumplings

¾ pound ground lean lamb
1 medium onion, finely chopped (about ½ cup)
¼ teaspoon ground cinnamon
Salt and freshly ground black pepper, to taste
3 tablespoons butter
½ recipe Griddle-Baked Pita, page 31, prepared through step 2
¼ cup pine nuts

Yogurt Soup

2 quarts yogurt, preferably homemade, page 32
1 tablespoon cornstarch
1 quart cold water
1 egg, beaten
1 teaspoon salt
3 tablespoons butter
1 large clove garlic, crushed
1 tablespoon finely chopped fresh mint or 1 teaspoon crumbled dried mint
Basic Pitas, page 21, cut into wedges

1. To prepare the dumplings, combine the lamb, onion, cinnamon, salt, and pepper in a small bowl. Melt the 3 tablespoons of butter in a large skillet. Add the lamb mixture and cook over medium heat, breaking it up as it cooks, until all the pink color has disappeared. Add the pine nuts and cook over high heat, stirring constantly, until lightly browned. Remove from the heat and let cool.

2. Divide the pita dough into 6 portions and shape into balls. Cover the balls with slightly damp towels, and let rest about 5 to 10 minutes.

3. Press each ball flat with your fingers, keeping it well rounded. Flour a work surface and rolling pin. Roll out each round to form a circle ⅛-inch thick. With a biscuit cutter, cut the dough into 2-inch circles. Repeat the process with the remaining dough, gathering up and combining any scraps, until you have 36 circles. Any remaining dough can be made into griddle-baked pitas, according to the recipe, page 31.

4. Top each circle with a little of the lamb mixture, dividing it evenly among the 36 circles. Fold each circle in half and pinch the edges firmly together. Bring the ends together and press the corners. See illustration.

5. To prepare the soup, put the yogurt into a large saucepan and whisk until it is thinned and smooth. In a small bowl, dissolve the cornstarch into ¼ cup of the cold water, then whisk it into the yogurt. Whisk in the beaten egg and blend thoroughly. Whisk in the remaining water and salt. Bring to a boil over medium heat, stirring constantly. When the yogurt mixture is boiling, drop in the dumplings, reduce the heat and simmer, covered, stirring occasionally, until the dumplings are tender, about 25 to 30 minutes.

6. Melt the butter in a skillet. Add the garlic and sauté over medium heat until softened and fragrant, about 3 minutes. Add to the soup. Stir in the mint and taste to correct seasonings. Serve immediately.

Makes 6 servings; 3 dozen dumplings.

Variation *Yogurt Soup with Middle Eastern Meatballs:* In addition to or instead of Pita Dumplings, add walnut-size Kibbeh, page 51.

Center filling on dough.

Fold dough over and pinch the edges closed.

Bring ends together and press to seal.

CHILLED CUCUMBER AND YOGURT SOUP

(Khyar Bi Laban)

Cucumbers and yogurt, seasoned with garlic and mint, appear in many forms throughout the East. Along the Mediterranean the combination is variously used as a sauce for dipping and lacing, as a salad dressing, and as a salad unto itself. In India, it is called raita and is served with curries as a topping or as an accompaniment. Here it stars as a zesty hot-weather soup to be served with garlicky Pita Crisps. Offer it as a first course to a Shish Kebab and pita meal, page 112. Always served icy cold, this soup can be made ahead and kept ready in the refrigerator.

2 quarts yogurt, preferably homemade, page 32
4 medium cucumbers, peeled, seeded, shredded, and drained
4 cloves garlic, crushed
Salt and freshly ground black pepper, to taste
1½ tablespoons chopped fresh mint or 1½ teaspoons crumbled dried mint
½ cup toasted pine nuts (garnish)
Garlic Pita Crisps, page 28

1. Put the yogurt into a large bowl and whisk until it is thinned and smooth.

2. Add the cucumbers, garlic, salt, pepper, and mint. Blend thoroughly. Taste to correct seasonings. Cover and refrigerate to chill.

3. Serve topped with a sprinkling of pine nuts, accompanied with garlic pita crisps.

Makes 8 servings.

SECRETS TO PREPARING SALAD AND SANDWICH GREENS

Salad greens play an important role in pita sandwiches and salads and should always be fresh and crisp. Greens make perfect liners for pita pockets and when shredded, offer a crunchy topping or serve as a base to catch a sauce or dressing.

The choice is wide in the market today: arugula, Belgian endive, chicory, cilantro, escarole, parsley, radicchio, cabbage, spinach, watercress, and the lettuces: Bibb, Boston, iceberg, red leaf, and romaine. Remember these few guidelines to their successful use:

● Wash and dry salad greens immediately after purchasing and refrigerate them as quickly as possible to insure the retention of a crisp texture, pleasing color, and good flavor.

● Drain all greens after washing them, shaking off as much water as possible, then blot them dry with paper towels.

● Store the washed greens in a vegetable crisper in the refrigerator. If you plan to store them for an extended period wrap them in dry paper towels, then place them in plastic bags.

● Remove bruised outer leaves on any head of lettuce. Leave the root ends on greens such as escarole, chicory, and romaine, and wash them thoroughly under running cold water.

● Greens with small leaves like cilantro, parsley, and watercress are best stored in tightly covered jars or plastic bags.

● Remove cleaned, crisped salad greens from the refrigerator about 1 hour before using and tear them into bite-size pieces. Tear the leaves gently to prevent them from discoloring. Return them to the refrigerator until serving time.

● Use dressing sparingly. Too much will make a salad wilt. I have given specific measurements for dressing ingredients in proportion to salad ingredients opting for lesser rather than greater amounts. On those occasions when you want to create a salad from scratch without a recipe, use ¼ cup of dressing for each 6 cups of greens. Toss gently, just until all the leaves are coated, not dripping. Once the salad is served, there should be no more than a teaspoon of dressing left in the bowl.

CAULIFLOWER, BROCCOLI, AND BELL PEPPER SALAD

Parboiled, yet crisp-tender cauliflower and broccoli florets teamed with strips of bright yellow and red bell peppers are laced with a Tahini dressing that has been delicately seasoned with garlic and generous squeezings of lemon juice. Serve this sophisticated combo with warm Sesame Pita wedges.

½ small head (about ½ pound) cauliflower, leaves trimmed, core removed, and cut into florets, parboiled, and drained
½ bunch (about ½ pound) broccoli, tops cut into florets, parboiled, and drained
1 small yellow bell pepper, cored, seeded and thinly sliced
1 small red bell pepper, cored, seeded and thinly sliced
1 clove garlic, crushed
¼ cup Tahini (sesame seed paste), page 41
¼ cup water
⅓ cup fresh lemon juice
Salt and freshly ground black pepper, to taste
Chopped fresh parsley, (garnish)
Sesame Pitas, page 22, cut into wedges

1. Place the cauliflower, broccoli, and yellow and red peppers in a medium salad bowl.

2. Whisk together the garlic, tahini, water, lemon juice, salt, and pepper in a small bowl.

3. Pour the dressing over the salad and toss gently to coat. Taste to correct seasonings. Refrigerate, covered, to chill. Serve on a platter. Garnish with the chopped parsley and surround with pita wedges.

Makes 6 servings.

Day-After-Thanksgiving Lunch

Turkey Salad Sesame in Whole-Wheat Honey Pitas topped with Cranberry Sauce
Carrot, Orange, and Radish Salad
Cauliflower and Onion Pickles
Pita Apple Crisps
Spiced Anise Tea

FETA CHEESE AND CUCUMBER SALAD

This easy-to-assemble salad is simply an arrangement of chopped cucumber and onion on a serving platter, topped with a blend of feta cheese, olive oil, yogurt, and lemon juice. It makes a marvelous accompaniment to *Kibbeh* (Middle Eastern Meatballs), page 51.

1 medium cucumber, peeled and chopped
1 small sweet onion, chopped
½ cup crumbled feta cheese
2 tablespoons olive oil
2 tablespoons yogurt, preferably homemade, page 32
1 tablespoon fresh lemon juice
Salt and freshly ground black pepper, to taste
Fresh mint, finely chopped, or crumbled dried mint (garnish)
Chopped scallions (garnish)
Poppy-Seed Pita Crisps, page 28

1. Arrange the cucumber and onion on a medium platter.

2. Place the feta cheese in a small bowl. Add the oil, yogurt, lemon juice, salt, and pepper. Mix thoroughly. Taste to correct seasonings.

3. Pour the dressing over the cucumber and onion. Garnish with the mint and scallions. Refrigerate, covered, to chill. Serve with poppy-seed pita crisps on the side.

Makes 4 servings.

CUCUMBER AND YOGURT SALAD

A classic Middle Eastern salad—you can put this together in moments.

2 cups yogurt, preferably homemade, page 32
1 small clove garlic, crushed
2 medium cucumbers, peeled and sliced
1 tablespoon chopped fresh mint
Salt and freshly ground black pepper, to taste

Herbed Zahter Pitas, page 26, cut into wedges

Combine all the ingredients except for the pita in a medium bowl and stir gently to blend. Taste to correct seasonings. Refrigerate, covered, to chill. Serve with zahter pita wedges.

Makes 3½ cups.

CARROT, ORANGE, AND RADISH SALAD

This spicy Moroccan salad, often served alongside couscous, is also a tempting topping for a chicken- or seafood-filled pita. The combination of orange and lemon juice adds a new twist to a basic dressing.

1 pound carrots, peeled and shredded
1 large orange, peeled, segmented, and cut into bite-size chunks
¾ cup thinly sliced radishes
½ cup finely chopped fresh cilantro
3 tablespoons olive oil
2 tablespoons fresh lemon juice
2 tablespoons fresh orange juice
Dash of orange-blossom water
Dash of ground cinnamon
Salt and freshly ground black pepper, to taste
Whole-Wheat Honey Pitas, page 23, cut into wedges

1. Combine the carrots, orange, radishes, and cilantro in a medium salad bowl.

2. Whisk together the olive oil, lemon juice, orange juice, orange-blossom water, cinnamon, salt, and pepper in a small bowl.

3. Pour the dressing over the salad and toss gently to coat. Taste to correct seasonings. Refrigerate, covered, to chill. Serve on a platter surrounded by pita wedges.

Makes 6 servings.

CLASSIC MEDITERRANEAN SALAD
(Salata)

Called *Salata,* meaning salad, this lovely toss of crisp lettuce, tomatoes, cucumbers, green pepper,

1 medium head romaine lettuce, leaves torn into bite-size pieces
3 small tomatoes, cut into wedges
1 medium cucumber, sliced
1 small green bell pepper, cored, seeded, and thinly sliced

1 small onion, cut into rings
6 radishes, thinly sliced
½ cup chopped fresh parsley
⅓ cup olive oil
3 tablespoons fresh lemon juice or more, to taste

onion, radishes, and parsley is traditionally served with almost every meal in the Middle East. Its piquant personality stems from a simple dressing of olive oil, lemon juice, and just the right amount of salt and pepper.

1 clove garlic, crushed
Salt and freshly ground black pepper, to taste
1 teaspoon crumbled dried mint
Poppy-seed Pitas page 22, cut into halves

1. Combine the lettuce, tomatoes, cucumber, green pepper, onion, radishes, and parsley in a large salad bowl.

2. Whisk together the olive oil, lemon juice, garlic, salt, pepper, and mint in a small bowl.

3. Pour the dressing over the salad and toss gently to coat. Taste to correct seasonings. Serve immediately with warm pita halves.

Makes 6 to 8 servings.

Variation *Chopped Vegetable Salad:* To serve as a topping for a pita sandwich or as an appetizer relish, omit the lettuce and chop all the vegetables into ½-inch dice. Toss with just enough dressing to season to taste.

TOMATO AND ONION SALAD

The classic Middle Eastern Tomato Salad is made with sliced sweet onion tossed gently with tomatoes and laced with a hefty serving of olive oil, lemon juice, and mint. Here, I've also added scallions, garlic, and cilantro. It is tasty alongside meat entrées, and is a piquant topping for Falafel, page 107.

6 medium tomatoes, cut into small wedges
4 scallions, chopped
1 small sweet onion, thinly sliced
2 tablespoons finely chopped fresh cilantro
1 tablespoon finely chopped fresh mint or 1 teaspoon crumbled dried mint
¼ cup olive oil
3 tablespoons fresh lemon juice
1 clove garlic, crushed
Salt and freshly ground black pepper, to taste
Poppy-seed Pitas, page 22, cut into wedges

1. Combine the tomatoes, scallions, onion, cilantro, and mint in a salad bowl.

2. Whisk together the oil, lemon juice, garlic, salt, and pepper in a small bowl.

3. Pour the dressing over the tomato mixture and toss gently to coat. Taste to correct seasonings. Refrigerate, covered, to chill. Serve with poppy-seed pita wedges.

Makes 6 to 8 servings.

CURRIED SPINACH, WALNUT, AND ORANGE SALAD

Crisp spinach leaves with crunchy walnuts and chunks of sweet orange fairly shimmer with a lacing of a curry-spiced dressing spiked with a dash of Ginger-Raisin Chutney. Serve this flavorful salad alongside a curry-filled pita pocket.

½ cup golden raisins
10 ounces fresh spinach, rinsed, and patted dry, stems trimmed, and leaves torn into bite-size pieces
3 scallions, chopped
1 large orange, peeled and diced
½ cup chopped walnuts
⅓ cup olive oil
3 tablespoons white wine vinegar
1 teaspoon sugar
½ teaspoon ground cumin
½ teaspoon Madras curry powder
Ginger-Raisin Chutney, to taste, page 137
Salt and freshly ground black pepper, to taste
Whole-Wheat Honey Pitas, page 23, cut into halves

1. Soak the raisins in boiling water until they are plumped, about 5 to 10 minutes. Drain thoroughly and dry with paper towels.

2. Combine the spinach, scallions, orange, walnuts, and raisins in a large salad bowl.

3. Whisk together the olive oil, vinegar, sugar, cumin, curry powder, chutney, salt and pepper.

4. Pour the dressing over the salad and toss gently to coat. Taste to correct seasonings. Serve immediately and surround with freshly made whole-wheat honey pita halves.

Makes 6 servings.

Autumn Back-Porch Supper

Oriental Shrimp and Black Bean Dip with Whole-Wheat Honey Pita wedges
Orange-Gingered Chicken in Poppy-Seed Pitas
Curried Spinach, Walnut and Orange Salad
Pistachio and Banana Toffee Rolls with Grand Marnier Syrup and Crème Fraîche
Mint Tea

MINTED POTATO SALAD

This chunky potato salad, rich in olive oil and lemon juice and the assertive flavor of mint, is a favorite accompaniment to the myriad lamb dishes of the Middle East. It goes particularly well with classic Shish Kebabs, page 112, especially for an outdoor barbecue. Make it several hours before serving as it tastes even better if it has had a chance to marinate a little. The Cabbage Salad variation is a sure-fire success when served as a topping for a Kefta Kebab in a pita, page 109.

6 cups (about 2½ pounds) diced, boiled small red potatoes
4 scallions, finely chopped
½ cup finely chopped fresh parsley
½ cup olive oil
⅓ cup fresh lemon juice
1 tablespoon chopped fresh mint or 1 teaspoon crumbled dried mint
Salt and freshly ground black pepper, to taste
Griddle-Baked Pitas, page 31

1. Combine the potatoes, scallions, and parsley in a large salad bowl.

2. Whisk together the olive oil, lemon juice, mint, salt, and pepper in a small bowl.

3. Pour the dressing over the salad and toss gently to coat. Taste to correct seasonings. Refrigerate, covered, to chill. When serving, offer griddle-baked pitas alongside.

Makes 6 servings.

Variation *Minted Cabbage Salad:* Substitute 6 cups shredded cabbage and 1 medium clove crushed garlic for the potatoes and scallions. Blend the crushed garlic with the olive oil, lemon juice, mint, salt, and pepper.

TABBOULEH

Tabbouleh, the famous bulgur salad of the Middle East, used variously as an appetizer, a topping for a pita sandwich, or as a dinner salad, has taken this country by storm. Now found in almost every deli section of supermarkets and gourmet food shops, this refreshing combination of bulgur, parsley, scallions, tomatoes, olive oil, and lemon juice is also simple to make at home. What follows is a classic recipe for you to use as a general guideline, but vary it to suit your personal taste! Many people like to add crushed garlic for added zest.

1 cup fine- to medium-grade bulgur
3 medium tomatoes, chopped
4 scallions, chopped
3 cups finely chopped fresh parsley
½ cup finely chopped fresh mint
½ cup olive oil
¼ to ⅓ cup fresh lemon juice, to taste
Salt and freshly ground black pepper, to taste
Romaine lettuce leaves
Whole-Wheat Honey Pitas, page 23, cut into halves

1. Rinse the bulgur and place it in a medium bowl. Cover with cool water and let soak until it is tender to the bite, 20 to 30 minutes. Drain thoroughly and squeeze out any excess water. Fluff to separate the grains.

2. Combine the tomatoes, scallions, parsley, and mint in a large salad bowl. Add the bulgur and toss gently.

3. Whisk together the olive oil, lemon juice, salt, and pepper in a small bowl.

4. Pour the dressing over the bulgur mixture and toss gently to coat. Taste to correct seasonings. Refrigerate, covered, to chill.

5. Line a salad bowl with lettuce leaves and arrange the tabbouleh on top. Offer whole-wheat honey pita halves on the side.

Makes 6 to 8 servings.

Tip

Try blending a sprinkling of cinnamon into the tabbouleh or pass cinnamon when serving.

BULGUR, FRUIT, AND CHEESE SALAD

This unusual meld of textures and flavors completely transforms the classic *tabbouleh*. Here crispy apples and romaine lettuce complement dates and cheese all nestled in tender bulgur grains and bathed in a honey-yogurt dressing. A complete meal when accompanied by warm pita, this salad without the cheese also makes a delightful accompaniment for chicken or seafood in a pita.

1 cup fine- to medium-grade bulgur
2 large firm Red Delicious apples, cored and diced
½ cup chopped dates
4 scallions, chopped
3 cups (about 1 medium head) shredded romaine lettuce
½ cup chopped fresh cilantro
½ cup chopped fresh parsley
⅓ cup olive oil
¼ cup fresh lemon juice
3 tablespoons yogurt, preferably homemade, page 32
1 tablespoon honey
½ teaspoon ground nutmeg
Salt and freshly ground black pepper, to taste
1 cup cubed muenster cheese
⅔ cup toasted slivered almonds
Wheat-Germ Honey Pitas, page 24, cut into halves

1. Rinse the bulgur and place it in a medium bowl. Cover with cool water and let soak until it is tender to the bite, 20 to 30 minutes. Drain thoroughly and squeeze out any excess water. Fluff to separate the grains.

2. Combine the apples, dates, scallions, lettuce, cilantro, and parsley in a large salad bowl. Add the bulgur and toss gently.

3. Whisk together the olive oil, lemon juice, yogurt, honey, nutmeg, salt, and pepper in a small bowl.

4. Pour the dressing over the bulgur mixture and toss gently to coat. Refrigerate, covered, to chill.

5. Just before serving, add the cheese and toasted almonds. Toss to combine and taste to correct seasonings. Serve with warm wheat-germ honey pita halves.

Makes 8 servings.

SPICY BULGUR SALAD

A first cousin to *Tabbouleh,* this bulgur salad is spiced with fresh cilantro, hot white radishes, and pungent fennel. Dress it all up with olive oil and lemon laced with cinnamon, cumin, and peppery cayenne and try serving it with little Coriander and Lamb Sausage patties, page 113, or Kefta Kebabs, page 109.

1 cup fine- to medium-grade bulgur
3 medium tomatoes, chopped
½ cup fennel, cut into julienne strips
1 cup chopped fresh parsley
2 tablespoons finely chopped fresh cilantro
½ cup (about 4 small) sliced hot white radishes
1 small head of romaine lettuce, leaves torn into bite-size pieces
4 scallions, chopped
½ cup olive oil
¼ to ⅓ cup fresh lemon juice
1 clove garlic, crushed
1 teaspoon ground cumin
½ teaspoon ground cinnamon
Dash of cayenne, or to taste
Salt and freshly ground black pepper, to taste
Basic Pitas, page 21, cut into halves

1. Rinse the bulgur and place it in a medium bowl. Cover with cool water and let soak until it is tender to the bite, 20 to 30 minutes. Drain thoroughly and squeeze out any excess water. Fluff to separate the grains.

2. Combine the tomatoes, fennel, parsley, cilantro, radishes, lettuce, and scallions in a large salad bowl. Add the bulgur and toss gently.

3. Whisk together the olive oil, lemon juice, garlic, cumin, cinnamon, cayenne, salt, and pepper in a small bowl.

4. Pour the dressing over the bulgur mixture and toss gently to coat. Taste to correct seasonings. Refrigerate, covered, to chill. Serve surrounded by warm pita halves.

Makes 6 servings.

ABOUT HERBS

When substituting dried herbs for fresh, use about ⅓ the amount; for example, 1 tablespoon of fresh chopped basil is equivalent to 1 teaspoon dried. Crumble dried herbs with your fingers to release their flavor.

PITA BREAD SALAD
(Fattoush)

Running a close second in popularity to *Tabbouleh,* in Middle Eastern homes is Pita Bread Salad or *Fattoush,* which translates as ''dampened or moist bread.'' I've given this version a Greek personality by adding some feta cheese and black Greek olives. Laced with a minted olive oil and lemon dressing and a sprinkling of *Zahter, Fattoush* is similar in character to a Caesar salad with the addition of crisp-toasted garlicky pita pieces. Add them last, of course, to preserve their crunchiness, and serve this salad alongside any meat, fish, or chicken-filled pita sandwich.

¼ cup butter, softened
2 cloves garlic, crushed
2 small Basic Pitas or 1 large, page 21
1 head of romaine lettuce, leaves torn into bite-size pieces
1 medium cucumber, peeled, sliced
6 scallions, chopped
2 medium tomatoes, cut into wedges
12 black Greek olives, pitted
⅔ cup crumbled feta cheese
½ cup chopped fresh parsley
⅓ cup olive oil, or more to taste
¼ cup fresh lemon juice, or more to taste
2 tablespoons chopped fresh mint
½ teaspoon zahter
Salt and freshly ground black pepper to taste

1. Preheat the broiler.

2. In a small bowl, cream the butter with 1 of the cloves of crushed garlic until blended.

3. Split the pitas into rounds and spread the insides with the garlic butter. Place on the broiler rack and toast until lightly browned. Turn off the oven and leave the bread inside until dry and crisp enough to break into bite-size pieces.

4. Combine the lettuce, cucumber, scallions, tomatoes, olives, feta, and parsley in a large salad bowl.

5. Whisk together the olive oil, lemon juice, remaining clove of crushed garlic, mint, zahter, salt, and pepper in a small bowl.

6. Pour the dressing over the salad and toss gently to coat. Add the toasted pita pieces and toss again. Taste to correct seasonings and serve immediately.

Makes 6 servings.

MARKET SALAD WITH BASIL TORTA VINAIGRETTE

This market basket full of fresh green vegetables marinated in pesto vinaigrette and tossed with diced basil torta and slivers of prosciutto is irresistible with freshly baked Whole-Wheat Honey Pitas.

2 medium carrots, peeled and cut into bite-size pieces
1 medium zucchini, cut into bite-size pieces
2 ribs celery, cut into bite-size pieces
1 package (10 ounces) frozen artichoke hearts, cooked and drained
1 cup small radishes, cut in half
1 cup snow peas, tips and strings removed
6 mushrooms, halved
½ cup chopped scallions
1 cup cherry tomatoes, halved
⅔ cup olive oil
1 small clove garlic, crushed
3 tablespoons fresh lemon juice
3 tablespoons Balsamic vinegar
1 tablespoon chopped fresh basil or 1 teaspoon crumbled dried basil
½ teaspoon dry mustard, optional
Salt and freshly ground black pepper, to taste
1 cup diced basil torta (see note)
8 thin slices prosciutto, slivered
Bibb lettuce leaves
Fresh basil leaves (garnish)
Black Greek olives, pitted (garnish)
Whole-Wheat Honey Pitas, page 23, cut into halves

1. Cook the carrots, zucchini, and celery in boiling salted water until crisp-tender, about 3 to 5 minutes. Drain and rinse under cold running water; drain well.

2. Combine the cooked vegetables with the artichoke hearts, radishes, snow peas, mushrooms, scallions, and tomatoes in a large salad bowl.

3. Whisk together the olive oil, garlic, lemon juice, vinegar, basil, mustard, salt, and pepper in a medium bowl.

4. Pour the dressing over the vegetables and toss gently to coat. Cover and marinate in the refrigerator for at least 1 hour.

5. Before serving, add the basil torta and prosciutto and toss. Taste to correct seasonings. Drain any excess dressing.

6. Served in chilled individual glass bowls lined with Bibb lettuce leaves. Sprinkle with basil leaves and olives. Pass baskets of warm pita.

Makes 8 servings.

Note: Basil torta is an appetizing cheese layered with basil and pine nuts. It is available in most cheese stores and in finer supermarkets.

CHEF'S COUSCOUS SALAD

To North Africans there is only one way to do *couscous*—steamed in a *couscousière* and served with a variety of vegetables, lamb, and chicken, then accompanied by a choice of sweet and tart salads and a good peppery hot sauce. Well, I won't disagree. But how about combining some cool crisp greens with fruit, vegetables, cold meats, and bulgur and coating them lightly with a zesty orange poppy-seed dressing. *Couscous?* Not quite, but surely a close cousin.

1 medium head romaine lettuce, leaves separated and torn into bite-size pieces
½ cup fine- to medium-grade bulgur
¾ cup golden raisins
1 cup cooked chickpeas (garbanzo beans), page 40
1 cup sliced radishes
2 cups julienned lean roasted lamb
1 whole cooked chicken breast, skinned, boned, and cut into julienne strips
1 orange, peeled, segmented, and cut into bite-size chunks
½ pound string cheese, pulled into strings
2 tablespoons fresh orange juice
2 tablespoons fresh lemon juice
⅓ cup olive oil
2 tablespoons honey
1 tablespoon poppy seeds
Salt and freshly ground black pepper, to taste
Wheat-Germ Honey Pitas, page 24, cut into wedges
Ginger-Raisin Chutney, page 137

1. Wrap the lettuce in paper towels and refrigerate to chill.

2. Rinse the bulgur and place it in a medium bowl. Cover with cool water and let soak until it is tender to the bite, 20 to 30 minutes. Drain thoroughly and squeeze out any excess water. Fluff to separate the grains.

3. Meanwhile, soak the raisins in boiling water until they are plumped, about 5 to 10 minutes. Drain thoroughly and dry with paper towels.

4. Combine the lettuce, bulgur, raisins, chickpeas, radishes, lamb, chicken, orange, and string cheese in a large salad bowl.

5. Whisk together the orange juice, lemon juice, olive oil, honey, poppy seeds, salt, and pepper.

6. Pour the dressing over the salad and toss gently to coat. Taste to correct seasonings. Refrigerate, covered, to chill.

7. Serve with warm wheat-germ honey pita wedges. Offer ginger-raisin chutney alongside for guests to add as they please.

Makes 8 servings.

PITA INSIDES

In America, pitas are most often stuffed to become a meal rolled up into one neat little menu-in-a-pocket.

The choices of what you can put in a pita are limitless. I've included a sampling of Middle Eastern classics such as *Shish Kebab* and *Falafel,* plus a variety of super salad sandwiches. In addition, there are loads of quick hot and cold deli sandwich ideas to get your creative juices flowing.

But that's not all. I've also created some wonderful curries for use especially with pitas—the sauces are thicker so they won't drip through the bread. To round off this section I have some eclectic dishes—from Pita Burritos to Gingered Tofu and Vegetable Toss—that draw from just about every ethnic heritage, and highlight just how versatile pita can be.

CLASSIC PARSLEY AND ONION OMELET
(Aijee)

This popular Mediterranean omelet is called *Aijee*. It can be prepared as a single, large, thick omelet similar to a frittata and cut into wedges for a cocktail appetizer or made into several small omelets to be served inside pitas.

8 eggs
1 tablespoon fresh lemon juice
¼ cup chopped fresh parsley
½ cup chopped scallions
1 tablespoon chopped fresh mint
Salt and freshly ground black pepper, to taste
3 tablespoons butter
Sesame Pitas, page 22, cut into wedges
Snipped fresh chives (garnish)
Chopped tomato (garnish)

1. Preheat the broiler.

2. Break the eggs into a large bowl. Add the lemon juice, and beat until light and foamy. Add the parsley, scallions, mint, salt, and pepper and blend well.

3. Melt the butter in a 10-inch ovenproof skillet. Add the egg mixture and cook over medium heat, carefully lifting the edges of the omelet to allow the uncooked eggs to run underneath, until the bottom is lightly browned, about 5 minutes.

Cover, lower the heat, and continue cooking until the top is completely set, 2 to 3 minutes.

4. Uncover the skillet and place under the broiler until the top is browned, 2 to 3 minutes. Remove from the broiler and cut into wedges. The omelet may be served either hot or cold. Place wedges of the omelet in the pita wedges and garnish with the chives and tomatoes.

Makes 4 to 6 servings.

Omelets are perfect fillings for medium-size pita halves. Make in a 6-inch omelet pan and fill them with your favorite goodies such as thinly sliced tomatoes, grated Swiss cheese, chopped parsley, basil and/or scallions. They nest snugly in the pocket for out-of-hand eating.

FALAFEL
(Chickpea Croquettes)

F*alafel*, enticing herbed croquettes popular as pushcart food all over the world, are as old as Middle Eastern cuisine itself. In Israel they are made with chickpeas or a combination of fava beans and chickpeas while in Egypt they are primarily made with fava beans and called *Taamiya*. If you like it hot, add a touch of Harissa, the Middle-Eastern answer to Salsa.

1½ cup dried chickpeas (garbanzo beans), cooked and drained (see page 40)
1 onion, chopped
¼ cup chopped fresh parsley
3 cloves garlic, crushed
1 egg
½ teaspoon baking soda
1 teaspoon ground coriander
1 teaspoon ground cumin
Salt and freshly ground black pepper, to taste
1 to 2 tablespoons unbleached all-purpose flour plus additional flour for coating patties
Vegetable oil, for frying
Small Basic Pitas, page 21, with the tops off
Chopped Vegetable Salad, page 95
Dash of Harissa (Hot Pepper Sauce), optional (recipe follows)

1. Place the chickpeas in a blender or food processor fitted with the metal blade. Add the onion, parsley, garlic, egg, baking soda, spices, salt, and pepper and process until smooth. Place in a glass bowl and refrigerate, covered, until firm, about 20 to 30 minutes.

2. Shape into 10 to 12 patties. Dust lightly on all sides with flour.

3. Pour the oil to a depth of ½ inch in a heavy skillet and heat until hot but not smoking. Working in batches, fry the patties turning frequently until browned and crisp, about 2 to 3 minutes. Drain on paper towels.

4. Put a croquette in each pita pocket. Top with chopped vegetable salad, and a little *harissa*. To store any remaining croquettes, refrigerate, covered, for up to 1 week.

Makes 10 to 12 patties.

Variations *Taratour Falafel:* Substitute shredded lettuce, chopped tomato, and scallions for the chopped vegetable salad and lace with Taratour, (sesame and garlic sauce), page 65.

Egyptian Bean Croquettes (Taamiya): Substitute fava beans (white broad beans) for the chickpeas in step 1. Fava beans impart more of a vegetable flavor than the nuttier chickpeas.

HARISSA
(Hot Pepper Sauce)

This hot pepper sauce, a native of North Africa, is often used to accompany couscous. Use a little as a dressing for pita sandwiches or as a dip with pita crisps.

½ pound hot red chiles, stemmed, seeded, and chopped
6 cloves garlic, peeled
1 teaspoon caraway seeds
1 teaspoon salt
1½ teaspoons freshly ground black pepper
1½ teaspoons ground cumin
1 teaspoon ground coriander
Olive oil

1. Place the peppers and garlic in a blender or food processor fitted with the metal blade. Process until coarsely ground.

2. Add the remaining ingredients except the olive oil and process until almost smooth. To store, place in a small jar, top with a thin layer of olive oil, and refrigerate until ready to use.

Makes about 1 cup.

Variation Add chopped roasted pepper or diced tomato to *Harissa* for variety.

KEFTA KEBABS

Kefta is a finely ground meat mixture much like our American hamburger but spiced with onion and parsley. It is shaped into sausage-like burgers on a skewer and broiled to a succulent turn. These are traditionally made in the Middle East with ground lamb, although beef seasoned in the same manner is equally good. I prefer lamb and find it easy to grind along with the other ingredients in a food processor. Use either the leg or shoulder. Cut out most of the fat and gristle, but leave a little fat to enhance the flavor.

1 pound lean ground lamb or beef
1 small onion, minced
3 tablespoons chopped fresh parsley
¼ teaspoon ground cinnamon
Dash of allspice
Salt and freshly ground black pepper, to taste
4 small Sesame Pitas, page 22, with the tops cut off
Shredded iceberg lettuce (garnish)
Chopped tomato (garnish)
Thinly sliced sweet onion (garnish)
Yogurt-Garlic Sauce, page 52

1.   Combine the lamb, onion, parsley, cinnamon, allspice, salt, and pepper in a large bowl; blend well. Refrigerate, covered, to chill until firm.

2.   Prepare a bowl of ice and water. Divide the mixture into 4 balls. Insert a metal skewer into the center of each ball. Dipping your hands into the bowl of ice and water to prevent the meat from sticking to them, mold each ball into a sausage shape around the skewer. Taper each end to secure the kebabs onto the skewers. (If desired, omit the skewers and mold the meat into rounded oval or flat patties.)

3.   Preheat the broiler.

4.   Place the skewers or patties on a broiler pan, about 2 to 3 inches from the heat. Broil, turning frequently, 5 to 6 minutes for rare, 7 to 8 minutes for medium, and 10 minutes for well done.

5.   To serve, put a kefta kebab in each pita pocket. Garnish with the shredded lettuce, chopped tomato, and sliced onion, and lace with Yogurt-Garlic Sauce.

Makes 4 kefta kebab sandwiches.

Note: To grill the kebabs over barbecue coals, first prepare the coals. Grill about 3 to 4 inches above the coals, turning frequently, 5 to 6 minutes for rare, 7 to 8 minutes for medium, and 10 minutes for well done.

Variation *Appetizer Meatball Kebabs:*   Divide the meat mixture into smaller balls. Arrange on skewers or pan fry, turning frequently, until evenly browned, about 10 minutes. Serve with *Taratour* (sesame and garlic sauce), page 65, and surround with fresh pita wedges.

Makes about 10 to 20 balls, depending on size.

GARLICKY SEAFOOD KEBABS

Mediterranean fishermen and cooks marinate these shrimp and scallops in super-garlicked olive oil and lemon juice seasoned with a dash of salt and a twist or two of freshly ground black pepper. These seafood and broccoli *kebabs* topped with *Taratour* and wrapped in a pita are simply luscious.

1½ pounds (about 18) large shrimp shelled and deveined
1½ pounds (about 18) sea scallops rinsed and drained
½ cup olive oil
¼ cup fresh lemon juice
2 cloves garlic, crushed
Salt and freshly ground black pepper, to taste
12 broccoli florets, parboiled
Taratour (sesame and garlic sauce), page 65
Griddle-Baked Pitas, page 31

1. Place the shrimp and scallops in a large shallow glass dish. Combine the oil, lemon juice, garlic, salt, and pepper in a small bowl. Blend well and pour over the seafood. Cover and marinate in the refrigerator, turning the pieces occasionally, for about 2 hours.

2. Preheat the broiler.

3. Remove the seafood from the marinade, reserving the marinade. Thread the shrimp, scallops, and broccoli florets evenly on 6 skewers.

4. Place the skewers on a broiler pan about 7 to 8 inches from the heat. Broil, turning frequently and basting with the reserved marinade, until the seafood is opaque, about 8 to 10 minutes.

5. Wrap a griddle-baked pita around each kebab and remove the skewer. Serve laced with Taratour.

Note: To grill the kebabs over barbecue coals, first prepare the coals. Thread the seafood and broccoli on skewers and grill 3 to 4 inches above the coals, turning frequently and basting with the reserved marinade, until the seafood is opaque, about 8 to 10 minutes.

Makes 6 servings.

THE FAMOUS YOGURT DRINK

All over the Middle East, in the Balkan countries, and in India, yogurt is widely acclaimed as a health-giving food and drink.

YOGURT PINEAPPLE COOLER

This almost, but not quite, sweet yogurt drink is especially good with a chicken, egg, or seafood salad-in-a-pita!

2 cups yogurt, preferably homemade, page 32
2 cups unsweetened pineapple juice
½ cup drained crushed pineapple
Mint sprigs (garnish)

Place the yogurt in a blender. Add the pineapple juice and crushed pineapple. Blend until smooth. Refrigerate, covered, to chill for at least 1 hour. Stir the yogurt mixture thoroughly just before serving and pour it into chilled tumblers. Garnish with the mint sprigs.

Variation *Fresh Fruit Shakes:* Substitute water or apple juice for the pineapple juice and add your favorite fresh fruits such as blueberries, peaches, strawberries, oranges, or bananas. Sweeten with honey or a dash of sugar, if desired.

SAVORY YOGURT AND MINT SHAKE WITH GARLIC

This zesty combo of yogurt and garlic, lightly seasoned with fresh mint is a lovely minty green cooler that is super served with a Garlicky Seafood Kebab in a Griddle-Baked Pita wrap.

2 cups yogurt, preferably homemade, page 32
2 cups ice water
1 clove garlic, cut in half
Salt, to taste
6 mint sprigs
Freshly ground black pepper (garnish)

Place the yogurt, water, garlic, salt, and 2 mint sprigs in a blender. Blend until smooth. Taste to correct seasonings. Refrigerate, covered, to chill for at least 1 hour. Stir the yogurt mixture thoroughly just before serving and pour it into chilled tumblers. Garnish with the remaining mint sprigs and a few twists of pepper.

Both fruit and savory yogurt shakes make 4 servings.

SHISH KEBABS

Shish Kebab simply means meat broiled on a skewer and it is traditionally cooked in this manner throughout the Middle East. At just about every street corner in New York City, there is a push-cart peddling meats grilled on bamboo skewers and served atop pitas, usually the flat Greek versions without pockets. I've marinated the lamb cubes in white wine blended with just the right amount of lemon and olive oil to enhance their delicate flavor. *Tabbouleh* is a natural companion.

2 pounds lamb, shoulder or leg, cut into 1½-inch cubes
1 cup dry white wine
¼ cup fresh lemon juice
½ cup olive oil
Salt and freshly ground black pepper, to taste
1 medium onion, sliced
2 cloves garlic, sliced
6 small white onions, cut in half
6 cherry tomatoes
1 large green bell pepper, cored, seeded, and cut into 12 chunks
6 medium Poppy-Seed Pitas, page 22, with the tops cut off

1. Place the lamb in a large, shallow, glass dish. Combine the wine, lemon juice, oil, salt, pepper, sliced onion, and garlic in a medium bowl. Blend well and pour over the lamb. Cover and marinate in the refrigerator, turning the lamb occasionally, for several hours or overnight. (The longer the lamb marinates, the more tender it becomes.)

2. Preheat the broiler.

3. Remove the lamb from the marinade, reserving the marinade. Thread the lamb, onion halves, cherry tomatoes, and green pepper chunks evenly on 6 skewers.

4. Place the skewers on a broiler pan about 2 to 3 inches from the heat. Broil, turning frequently and basting with the reserved marinade, 5 to 7 minutes for rare, 8 to 10 minutes for medium, and 12 to 15 minutes for well done.

5. To serve, remove the lamb cubes and vegetables from the skewers and put them in the pita pockets while they are still warm.

Makes 6 servings.

Note: To grill the kebabs over barbecue coals, first prepare the coals, then thread the lamb on the skewers without the vegetables. Grill 4 to 5 inches above the coals, turning frequently and basting with the reserved marinade, 5 to 7 minutes for rare, 8 to 10 minutes for medium, and 12 to 15 minutes for well done.

To grill the vegetables, thread the onions and peppers on 1 skewer. Thread the tomatoes on a second skewer. Grill 4 to 5 inches above the coals, turning frequently and basting with the reserved marinade, 15 to 18 minutes for the onions and peppers, about 5 to 8 minutes for the tomatoes.

Variation *Shish Kebab in Yogurt Marinade:* Substitute Yogurt Marinade for the oil and lemon marinade above: Combine 1 cup yogurt (preferably homemade, page 32), 1 or 2 crushed garlic cloves, 1 small minced onion, 1 teaspoon ground coriander, and ½ teaspoon crum-bled dried mint in a small bowl. Blend thoroughly and pour the marinade over the lamb. Cover and refrigerate as above.

CORIANDER AND LAMB SAUSAGE PATTIES
(Mahnik)

These succulent little lamb sausages are simple to make and a treat to eat! I've added just enough fat to make them tasty and moist, although if you want a completely low-fat sausage, simply omit the fat. Slipped into a pita pocket with herb-scrambled eggs, they are an excellent brunch or breakfast offering. They also make a hearty sandwich when accompanied by a Classic Mediterranean Salad, page 94.

2 pounds ground lean lamb
½ cup ground lamb fat (optional)
½ cup hearty red wine
¼ cup whole coriander seeds
1 teaspoon ground coriander
½ teaspoon allspice
½ teaspoon ground cinnamon
Salt and freshly ground black pepper, to taste
Vegetable oil, for frying
Griddle-Baked Pitas, page 31

1. Mix together the ground lamb and lamb fat in a large shallow glass dish. Combine the remaining ingredients except the pita in a small bowl. Blend well and pour over the lamb. Cover and marinate in the refrigerator, turning the pieces occasionally, for 3 hours. Remove the lamb from the marinade.

2. Shape 1 rounded tablespoon of the meat into a small patty. Lightly grease a heavy skillet and pan fry the patty over medium heat until browned on both sides. Taste the cooked patty and correct any seasonings in the uncooked meat.

3. Form the remaining meat into twelve 2-inch patties or small sausage-like rolls. (The patties can be made ahead to this point and frozen for up to 3 months in small freezer-proof plastic bags, separating each patty with a piece of plastic wrap. Some wine will seep into the bag and serve as a marinade.)

4. Working in two batches, lightly grease a heavy skillet and pan fry the patties over medium heat until browned on both sides, about 8 to 10 minutes. Drain on paper towels.

5. Serve warm, wrapped in griddle-baked pitas.

Makes 12 patties or rolls.

HERB-BROILED CHICKEN AND ONION ON A PITA

Throughout the Middle East, street or *souk* vendors sell savory herbed chicken atop zahter-seasoned pitas. While they season both the chicken and the pita with zahter, I've departed from tradition by offering broiled chicken marinated in olive oil, wine, and thyme, and served with an onion-pine nut sauté atop Herbed Zahter Pitas. Served cold, it makes a wonderful picnic packet, wrapped individually in aluminum foil. I prefer it hot, however, when all the oils and juices combine to make the chicken superbly succulent. This is a marvelous dish for an outdoor barbecue (see note).

2 chickens (about 2½ to 3 pounds each), cut into quarters
1 cup olive oil
¼ cup dry white wine
1 large clove garlic, crushed
¾ teaspoon crumbled dried thyme
Salt and freshly ground black pepper, to taste
4 medium onions, sliced
¼ cup pine nuts
8 Herbed Zahter Pitas, page 26

1. Lay the chicken quarters in a large glass or pottery baking dish. Combine ¾ cup of the oil, the wine, garlic, thyme, salt, and pepper in a small bowl. Blend well and pour over the chicken. Cover and marinate in the refrigerator, turning the pieces occasionally, for several hours or overnight.

2. Preheat the broiler.

3. Remove the chicken from the marinade, reserving the marinade. Broil, skinside down, 7 to 8 inches from the heat for about 30 minutes. Turn and brush with the marinade. Broil until tender, 15 to 30 minutes longer.

4. Meanwhile, heat the remaining oil in a large skillet. Add the onions and pine nuts and sauté over medium heat until the onions are light yellow and the pine nuts are golden, about 8 to 10 minutes.

5. Spoon some of the onion and nut mixture on the tops of the pitas. Top each with a broiled chicken quarter.

Makes 8 servings.

Note: To grill over barbecue coals, first prepare the coals. Place the chicken on the grill, skinside down, 6 to 7 inches above the coals. Grill until the skin is golden brown, about 10 minutes. Brush with the marinade. Turn and grill 20 to 30 minutes longer. Brush again with the marinade and turn, grilling 5 minutes longer on each side or until chicken is tender and crisp. Turn frequently to ensure a golden-brown surface without burning and charring the skin.

COLD PITA DELIS

Pitas make absolutely delicious deli sandwiches. Try these dandy combos.

PITA CLUB

Spread the insides of a Basic Pita with mayonnaise and fill it with cold sliced chicken, bacon slices, thinly sliced tomato, and romaine lettuce leaves. Top it all off with freshly ground black pepper.

ROAST BEEF WITH ONION

Spread a thin coating of Russian dressing on the insides of a Sesame Pita and line it with paper-thin slices of rare roast beef, tomato, sweet pickles, and sweet red onion.

SHRIMP SALAD AND SESAME

Line a Whole-Wheat Honey Pita with Bibb lettuce and fill it with shrimp salad, sliced artichoke hearts, and chopped scallions. Crown it with a sprinkling of toasted sesame seeds.

CHICKEN SALAD WITH YOGURT CHEESE AND BLACK OLIVES

Spread the insides of a Wheat-Germ Honey Pita with yogurt cheese. Fill with chicken salad sprinkled with chopped almonds. Top it with chopped black Greek Olives.

LIVERWURST, SLICED EGG, AND SCALLIONS

Season the insides of a Basic Pita with a mustardy mayonnaise and layer thin slices of liverwurst and hard-cooked egg sprinkled with chopped scallions. Add some crisp romaine lettuce leaves.

TOFU, AVOCADO, AND ALFALFA SPROUTS

Spread the insides of a Wheat-Germ Honey Pita with a thyme-seasoned mayonnaise and fill it with chopped tofu and shredded Swiss cheese. Add sliced avocado and mushrooms topped with alfalfa sprouts and a dollop of the seasoned mayonnaise.

EGG SALAD WITH TARATOUR

Mound egg salad in a Sesame Pita, lace it with Taratour (sesame and garlic sauce) and sprinkle with toasted sesame seeds.

CHICKEN SALAD SESAME

There are probably as many varieties of chicken salad as there are chickens in the world, but I think this recipe is particularly tasty. The addition of Tahini and yogurt gives it a piquant nutty verve. Fill pitas with this unusual mix and garnish with toasted sesame seeds.

3 cups cooked diced chicken
1 cup diced celery
1 cup seedless green grapes, cut in half
½ cup toasted pine nuts
⅓ cup mayonnaise
¼ cup yogurt, preferably homemade, page 32
2 tablespoons Tahini (sesame seed paste), page 41
Salt and freshly ground black pepper, to taste
Small Sesame Pitas, page 22, with the tops cut off
Romaine lettuce leaves
Toasted sesame seeds (garnish)
Additional grape halves (garnish)

1. Combine the chicken, celery, grapes, and pine nuts in a large bowl.

2. Whisk together the mayonnaise, yogurt, tahini, salt, and pepper in a small bowl.

3. Fold the dressing into the chicken salad and toss gently to coat. Taste to correct seasonings. Refrigerate, covered, to chill.

4. Line the pitas with the lettuce leaves and fill with the chicken salad. Garnish with toasted sesame seeds and additional grape halves.

Makes about 5½ cups.

Spring Terrace Luncheon

White wine spritzers with kiwi and orange slices
Oriental Shrimp and Black Bean Dip with Whole-Wheat Honey Pita wedges
Chicken Salad Sesame in Sesame Pitas
Dilled Cucumber-Salmon Salad in Wheat-Germ Honey Pitas
Pita Bread Salad
Sweet Pita Crisps with Sesame-Honey, Sesame-Carob, and Sesame-Maple Dipping Sauces
Mint Tea

CHICKEN SALAD BEARNAISE

If you like traditional Steak Béarnaise, you'll adore this Chicken Salad Béarnaise. The mixture of diced chicken, celery, scallions, raisins, and almonds is dressed in a delicate toss of tarragon-seasoned mayonnaise, parsley, and white wine. In a pita pocket lined with iceberg lettuce leaves and topped with sliced black olives, it's scrumptious!

½ cup raisins
2½ cups cooked diced chicken
1 cup diced celery
2 scallions, finely chopped
½ cup toasted slivered almonds
½ cup mayonnaise
1 tablespoon dry white wine
¼ cup chopped parsley
1 teaspoon chopped fresh tarragon or ½ teaspoon crumbled dried tarragon
Salt and freshly ground black pepper, to taste
Small Whole-Wheat Sesame Pitas, page 24, with the tops cut off
Iceberg lettuce leaves
Sliced black Greek olives (garnish)

1. Soak the raisins in boiling water until they are plumped, about 5 to 10 minutes. Drain thoroughly and dry with paper towels.

2. Combine the raisins, chicken, celery, scallions, and almonds in a large bowl.

3. Whisk together the mayonnaise, wine, parsley, tarragon, salt, and pepper in a small bowl.

4. Fold the dressing into the chicken salad and toss gently to coat. Taste to correct seasonings. Refrigerate, covered, to chill.

5. Line the pitas with the lettuce leaves. Fill with the chicken salad and top with sliced olives.

Makes about 4 cups.

SMOKED TURKEY AND APRICOT SALAD

The sweet and smoky blend of turkey and apricot tossed in a celery-seed mayonnaise makes a perfect filling for Wheat-Germ Honey Pitas.

2 cups julienned smoked turkey
1 cup chopped celery
½ cup finely chopped dried
    apricots
¼ cup finely chopped sweet pickles
½ cup thinly sliced radishes
2 scallions, chopped
½ cup mayonnaise
1 teaspoon celery seed
Salt and freshly ground black
    pepper, to taste
Small Wheat-Germ Honey Pitas,
    page 24, with the tops cut off
Shredded romaine lettuce

1. Combine the turkey, celery, apricots, pickles, radishes, and scallions in a large bowl.

2. Whisk together the mayonnaise, celery seed, salt, and pepper in a small bowl.

3. Fold the dressing into the turkey salad and toss gently to coat. Taste to correct seasonings. Refrigerate, covered, to chill.

4. Line the pitas with the shredded lettuce and fill with the turkey salad.

Makes about 4 cups.

Late Summer Buffet Luncheon

Herbed Bloody Marys with
    fresh cilantro sprigs
Hummus Guacamole with
    Parmesan Pita Crisps
Scallop and Melon-Ball Salad
    in Basic Pitas
Smoked Turkey and Apricot
    Salad in Wheat-Germ Honey
    Pitas
Cauliflower, Broccoli, and
    Bell-Pepper Salad
Spiced Apple Pudding with
    Vanilla Sauce
Iced Mint Tea

CHICKEN BROCCOLI DIVAN

In this favorite recipe from my good friend Marian Stamos of Chicago, a touch of sherry spices up a classic chicken salad while the broccoli offers a sure-fire bounce in texture, color, and vitamins.

2 cups cooked diced chicken
1¼ cups cooked chopped broccoli
⅓ cup chopped celery
½ cup mayonnaise
1 tablespoon dry sherry
1 teaspoon Dijon-style mustard
½ teaspoon salt
½ teaspoon Worcestershire sauce
Small Basic Pitas, page 21, with the tops cut off
Shredded Bibb lettuce

1. Combine the chicken, broccoli, and celery in a large bowl.

2. Whisk together the mayonnaise, sherry, mustard, salt, and Worcestershire sauce in a small bowl.

3. Fold the dressing into the chicken salad and toss gently to coat. Taste to correct seasonings. Refrigerate, covered, to chill.

4. Line the pitas with the shredded lettuce and fill them with the chicken salad.

Makes about 4 cups.

PEANUT BUTTER AND PITA

Peanut butter is marvelous in pitas and you can vary its personality with the addition of a host of delicious ingredients. First cut medium pitas in half and spread the pockets with your favorite brand of peanut butter. Then try some of the following additions to make a special lunch box or picnic treat for children of all ages.

- Raisins and pecans
- Apples and walnuts
- Bananas and raisins
- Crumbled bacon
- Shredded carrots, raisins, and almonds
- Alfalfa sprouts, chopped dates, and macadamia nuts
- Homemade applesauce or whole cranberry sauce
- Sliced green or red bell pepper
- Homemade grape or blackberry preserves

CRABMEAT, CARROT, AND GRAPE SALAD

This healthy, healthy salad tastes just as good as it is good for you!

2 cups (about 1 pound) shelled cooked crabmeat
1 cup diced celery
2 scallions, finely chopped
1 tablespoon finely chopped fresh parsley
1 carrot, peeled and grated
1 cup seedless green grapes, cut in half
½ cup mayonnaise
¼ cup yogurt, preferably homemade, page 32
1 teaspoon fresh lemon juice
1 teaspoon fresh orange juice
Salt and freshly ground black pepper, to taste

Dash of Harissa (Hot Pepper Sauce), optional, page 108
Small Whole-Wheat Honey Pitas, page 24, with the tops cut off
Belgian endive leaves

1. Combine the crabmeat, celery, scallions, parsley, carrot, and grapes in a large bowl.

2. Whisk together the mayonnaise, yogurt, lemon juice, orange juice, salt, pepper, and harissa, if desired, in a small bowl.

3. Fold the dressing into the crabmeat salad and toss gently to coat. Taste to correct seasonings. Refrigerate, covered, to chill.

4. Line the pitas with the endive and fill with the crabmeat salad.

Makes about 4 cups.

CRABMEAT AND NUT HAWAIIAN SALAD

Fruit in combination with seafood is enhanced with a light curry mayonnaise. What makes this salad especially good is a blend of macadamia nuts, pineapple, and avocado. Add a touch of papaya instead of the avocado for a change of pace!

2 cups (about 1 pound) shelled cooked crabmeat
½ cup diced celery
1 cup ripe fresh pineapple chunks, cut in ½-inch cubes or 1 can (8 ounces) pineapple chunks, drained and cut in ½-inch cubes
½ ripe avocado, pitted, peeled, and thinly sliced
½ cup mayonnaise
¼ cup yogurt, preferably homemade, page 32
½ teaspoon Madras curry powder, or to taste
Salt and freshly ground black pepper, to taste
½ cup coarsely chopped macadamia nuts
Small Whole-Wheat Honey Pitas, page 23, with the tops cut off
Shredded red leaf lettuce

1. Combine the crabmeat, celery, pineapple, and avocado in a large bowl.

2. Whisk together the mayonnaise, yogurt, curry powder, salt, pepper, and half of the macadamia nuts in a small bowl.

3. Fold the dressing into the crabmeat salad and toss gently to coat. Taste to correct seasonings. Refrigerate, covered, to chill.

4. Line the pitas with the shredded lettuce and fill with the crabmeat salad. Sprinkle with the remaining macadamia nuts.

Makes about 4 cups.

Lunch at the Beach

Crudités (carrot curls, celery sticks, zucchini circles) with Yogurt-Garlic Dip
Down-East Lobster Rolls in Basic Pitas
Crabmeat and Nut Hawaiian Salad in Whole-Wheat Honey Pitas
Pressed Apricot Rolls
Orangeade with orange-blossom water

GRILLED DELI PITAS

Fill pitas with any of the following delicious combinations. Spread the outsides with softened butter and grill them on a lightly greased skillet or sandwich grill until they are lightly browned and slightly crisp.

SWISS CHEESE, YELLOW BELL PEPPER, AND COUNTRY HAM

Mound grated Swiss cheese, thinly sliced tomatoes, slivers of yellow bell pepper, and sliced mushrooms in a Whole-Wheat Honey Pita. Top it with paper-thin slices of country ham lightly spread with a spicy mustard.

SAUTEED LAMB SAUSAGE AND STRING CHEESE

Sauté crumbled Coriander and Lamb Sausage, page 113, with chopped garlic and onion. Stuff in a Sesame Pita and top with a hefty measure of string cheese and finely chopped black Greek olives.

CUBAN CAFETERIA GRILL

Layer thinly sliced smoked ham, roast fresh pork, Swiss cheese, and sliced dill pickles in a Basic Pita and slather it all with a light spread of prepared yellow mustard.

KASSERI CHEESE, PROSCIUTTO, AND ZUCCHINI

Drizzle the insides of a Poppy-Seed Pita with olive oil and a light sprinkling of chopped fresh basil, then layer thin slices of Kasseri cheese, prosciutto, and zucchini topped with chopped scallions.

APPLE, BLUE CHEESE, AND SMOKED TURKEY

Spread the insides of a Wheat-Germ Honey Pita with softened butter and sprinkle lightly with freshly ground black pepper. Layer thinly sliced apples and smoked turkey topped with crumbled blue cheese.

SWISS CHEESE AND MAPLE SYRUP BRUNCH SANDWICH

Mound grated Swiss cheese inside a Sesame Pita and top with crisp bacon slices. Serve with warm pure maple syrup after removing the sandwich from the grill.

SCALLOP AND MELON-BALL SALAD

This unusual mingle of ingredients creates a pleasingly refreshing pita sandwich filling. The toasted sunflower seeds add the crowning touch.

1 pound sea scallops, rinsed and drained
3 scallions, finely chopped
½ cup dry white wine
½ teaspoon salt
1 tablespoon fresh lime juice
½ cup chopped celery
1 cup diced cantalope or crenshaw melon, cut into bite-size pieces
1 tablespoon finely chopped fresh cilantro
½ cup mayonnaise
¼ cup yogurt, preferably homemade, page 32
Salt and freshly ground black pepper, to taste
½ cup toasted sunflower seeds
Small Basic Pitas, page 21, with the tops cut off
Bibb lettuce leaves
Sliced pitted black California olives (garnish)

1. Place the scallops, ⅓ of the chopped scallions, and the wine in a skillet. Pour in enough water to just cover. Add the salt and bring to a boil. Reduce the heat and simmer, uncovered, until the scallops begin to change color, about 1 minute.

Remove from the heat and let the scallops cool in the poaching liquid; drain and discard the poaching liquid. Cut them into ½-inch pieces.

2. Place the scallops in a large bowl and sprinkle with the lime juice. Add the remaining scallions, the celery, melon, and cilantro. Toss gently to blend.

3. Whisk together the mayonnaise, yogurt, salt, and pepper in a small bowl.

4. Fold the dressing into the scallop salad and toss gently to coat. Refrigerate, covered, to chill.

5. Just before serving add the sunflower seeds and toss again. Taste to correct seasonings.

6. Line the pitas with the lettuce leaves and fill with the scallop salad. Sprinkle with the sliced black olives.

Makes about 4½ cups.

CURRIED SHRIMP, PERSIMMON, AND NUT SALAD

The flavorful combination of shrimp, persimmon, and apple is heightened with the addition of curry, pecans, and poppy seeds. This makes a perfect transitional sandwich offering for the fall and winter months when persimmons are at their sweet luscious peak. To avoid any mouth-puckering bitterness, be sure to choose ripe persimmons—they'll be a deep orange and soft.

2 pounds cooked medium shrimp
½ cup chopped celery
2 ripe persimmons, seeded, peeled, and chopped (they'll be slightly mashed)
1 Golden Delicious apple, chopped
½ cup mayonnaise
¼ cup yogurt, preferably homemade, page 32
1 teaspoon Madras curry powder
Salt and freshly ground black pepper, to taste
½ cup chopped pecans
¼ cup poppy seeds
Small Whole-Wheat Honey Pitas, page 23, with the tops cut off
Shredded iceberg lettuce

1. Combine the shrimp, celery, persimmons, and apple in a large bowl.

2. Whisk together the mayonnaise, yogurt, curry powder, salt, pepper, pecans, and poppy seeds in a small bowl.

3. Fold the dressing into the shrimp salad and toss gently to coat. Taste to correct seasonings. Refrigerate, covered, to chill.

4. Line the pitas with the shredded lettuce and fill with the shrimp salad.

Makes about 5 cups.

DOWN-EAST LOBSTER ROLL IN A PITA

This Down-East tradition makes a perfect filling for a pita.
Blend 1 pound of freshly cooked lobster meat, cut in chunks, with 3 tablespoons of mayonnaise and refrigerate, covered, to chill. Meanwhile, cut the tops off 4 Basic Pitas, spread the insides with melted butter, wrap them in aluminum foil, and place them in a preheated 300°F until just warm, 3 to 5 minutes. Fill them with the lobster salad, sprinkle with chopped fresh parsley, and serve immediately with a tall glass of fresh lemonade! Pass lemon wedges for those seafood-with-lemon devotees!

DILLED CUCUMBER-SALMON SALAD

Cucumber and salmon are favorite teammates and here the addition of yogurt binds them closer together. The sprinkling of dill assures a perfect marriage.

2 cucumbers, peeled, halved
*   lengthwise, seeded, and thinly*
*   sliced*
Salt and freshly ground black
*   pepper, to taste*
2 cups flaked cooked salmon, or 1
*   can (1 pound) salmon, drained*
*   and flaked*
½ cup yogurt, preferably
*   homemade, page 32*
Fresh lemon juice, to taste

½ cup chopped celery
1 large scallion, finely chopped
1 tablespoon finely chopped fresh
*   dill or 1 teaspoon dried dill*
Small Wheat-Germ Honey Pitas,
*   page 24, with the tops cut off*
Bibb lettuce leaves
Additional finely chopped fresh dill
*   (garnish)*

1. Place the cucumbers in a colander set over a medium bowl. Sprinkle lightly with salt and pepper and toss to mix. Set aside until wilted, about 15 to 20 minutes. Squeeze out the water and pat dry with paper towels.

2. Transfer the cucumbers into a large bowl. Add the salmon, yogurt, lemon juice, celery, scallion, and dill. Toss gently to blend. Taste to correct seasonings. Refrigerate, covered, to chill.

3. Line the pitas with the lettuce leaves and fill with the cucumber-salmon salad. Garnish with the extra dill.

Makes 3½ cups.

NOPALITO CACTUS, TOMATO, AND FETA SALAD

I've adapted this delightful recipe from one given to me by my good friends Edward and M'Lou Holliday in Key Biscayne, Florida. They use fresh nopal cactus from the garden, cleaned, with the thorns removed, cooked briefly in boiling salted water, then refrigerated. (Before you use either fresh or canned nopalitos, be sure to rinse and drain them thoroughly in order to remove the natural thick residue.) They serve their nopalito salad rolled in tortillas as an appetizer, but it is equally delicious in griddle-baked pitas, topped with feta cheese and jalapeño chiles. Guaranteed to arouse questions and raves!

2 cups (two 8-ounce cans) nopalitos, rinsed and drained
2 medium tomatoes, seeded and chopped
1 small onion, finely chopped
2 tablespoons chopped fresh cilantro
3 tablespoons olive oil
1 tablespoon red wine vinegar
¼ teaspoon crumbled dried oregano
Salt and freshly ground black pepper, to taste
Griddle-Baked Pitas, page 31
Romaine lettuce leaves
Strips of seeded fresh jalapeño chiles (garnish)
Crumbled feta cheese (garnish)
Chopped fresh cilantro (garnish)

1. Combine the cactus, tomatoes, onion, and cilantro in a large bowl.

2. Whisk together the olive oil, vinegar, oregano, salt, and pepper in a small bowl.

3. Pour the dressing over the cactus salad and toss gently to coat. Taste to correct seasonings. Refrigerate, covered, to chill.

4. Top the griddle-baked pitas with the lettuce leaves followed by the cactus salad. Garnish with the chile strips. Sprinkle with feta cheese and cilantro. Roll the pitas closed and serve each in squares of parchment paper to catch any drips.

Makes about 3½ cups.

SMOKED HAM AND FRESH ASPARAGUS

This refreshing sandwich comes alive with crisp-tender fresh asparagus marinated in a piquant minted oil-and-lemon dressing. Serve it with fresh yogurt cheese and smoked ham and top it with radicchio. A perfect celebration when the first young asparagus shoots hit the spring market!

24 asparagus spears, cooked until crisp-tender
Freshly ground black pepper, to taste
½ cup olive oil
¼ cup fresh lemon juice
1 teaspoon finely chopped fresh mint
Salt, to taste
12 thin slices of smoked ham
6 small Wheat-Germ Honey Pitas, page 24, with the tops cut off
¾ to 1 cup Yogurt Cheese, page 33
Shredded radicchio

1. Trim the asparagus spears to fit inside the pitas then place the spears in a glass or pottery dish. Sprinkle with the pepper.

2. Whisk together the olive oil, lemon juice, mint, salt, and pepper in a small bowl. Pour the dressing over the asparagus. Cover and marinate in the refrigerator, turning the spears occasionally, for 2 hours.

3. Drain the asparagus, reserving the marinade. Roll 2 asparagus spears in each slice of the smoked ham. Set the rolls aside.

4. Spread the insides of the pitas with the yogurt cheese, dividing it evenly among the 6 loaves. Place two roll-ups in each pita. Top with the shredded radicchio and drizzle a little of the reserved marinade over everything.

Makes 6 sandwiches.

Summer Picnic

Herbed Hummus with Pistachios and Poppy-Seed Pita wedges
Spinach and Raisin Triangles
Smoked Ham and Fresh Asparagus in Wheat-Germ Honey Pitas
Marinated Artichokes with Salonika Peppers
Pressed Apricot Rolls
Chilled white wine
Iced Mint Tea

DEVILED EGG AND MUSHROOM SALAD

The mushrooms and shallots must be sautéed first, then laced with white wine and simmered until all the wine and water from the mushrooms has evaporated before the unique flavor of this egg salad reaches its peak.

2 tablespoons butter
½ pound mushrooms, wiped clean with damp paper towels, and chopped
2 tablespoons chopped shallots
2 tablespoons dry white wine
6 hard-cooked eggs, chopped
½ cup chopped celery
½ cup mayonnaise
2 tablespoons yogurt, preferably homemade, page 32
1 tablespoon Dijon-style mustard
Salt and freshly ground black pepper, to taste
Small Basic Pitas, page 21, with the tops cut off
Alfalfa sprouts (garnish)
Snipped fresh chives (garnish)

1. Melt the butter in a large skillet. Add the mushrooms and shallots and sauté over medium heat until tender, about 5 minutes. Add the wine and cook over low heat until all the liquid has evaporated. Remove from the heat and let cool. Refrigerate, covered, to chill.

2. Place the chopped eggs in a medium bowl. Add the celery, and cooled mushrooms and shallots.

3. Whisk together the mayonnaise, yogurt, mustard, salt, and pepper in a small bowl.

4. Fold the dressing into the egg mixture and toss gently to coat. Taste to correct seasonings. Refrigerate, covered, to chill.

5. Fill the pitas with the egg salad and garnish with alfalfa sprouts and chives.

Makes about 2 cups.

OPEN-FACED PITA CHEESE MELTS

Turn a thin loaf of pita bottom side up or split thicker loaves in two, spread with softened butter, a favorite dressing, and top off with a combination of special sandwich fillings and cheese. Broil it all to a bubbly turn for a super-duper open-faced pita cheese melt.

SALMON SALAD WITH CURRIED MAYONNAISE

Spread Sesame Whole-Wheat Pita with curried mayonnaise and mound it with salmon salad. Top it with chopped scallions and grated Jarlsberg cheese, sprinkled with freshly snipped dill and a squeeze of lemon juice.

REUBEN WITH GARLICKY DILL

Spread a Wheat-Germ Honey Pita with Dijon-style mustard and top it with thinly sliced, lean corned beef, drained sauerkraut sprinkled with caraway seeds, thinly sliced garlicky dill pickles, and grated Swiss cheese.

MIDDLE-EASTERN NACHO MELT

Spread a Sesame Pita with *Hummus Bi Tahini*. Top it with chopped fresh cilantro, sliced Salonika peppers, crumbled feta cheese, and grated Kasseri cheese.

BLACK FOREST HAM, FONTINA, AND PINEAPPLE

Blend a little Dijon-style mustard with brown sugar and a dash of cloves and spread it on a Whole-Wheat Honey Pita. Layer on thinly sliced Black Forest ham, and top it with strained crushed pineapple squeezed to remove excess moisture, and sliced Fontina cheese.

CURRIED TUNA SALAD, WATERCRESS, AND CHEDDAR CHEESE

Top a Basic Pita with Curried Tuna Salad laced with chopped watercress and slivered Cheddar cheese.

STRING CHEESE, FRUIT, AND NUT SALAD

String cheese, a mild, braided Middle Eastern cheese seasoned with crushed black cherry kernels and whole black caraway seeds, is marvelous tossed together with fruit in a sesame mayonnaise.

½ pound seedless green grapes, cut in half
1 large green apple, cut into bite-size pieces
½ pound string cheese, separated and pulled into strings
¼ cup mayonnaise
¼ cup Tahini (sesame seed paste), page 41
2 tablespoons toasted sesame seeds, page 165
1 tablespoon fresh lemon juice
½ cup toasted pine nuts, page 164
Small Sesame Pitas, page 22, with the tops cut off
Chicory leaves

1.   Combine the grapes, apple, and string cheese in a large bowl.

2.   Whisk together the mayonnaise, tahini, toasted sesame seeds, and lemon juice in a small bowl.

3.   Fold the dressing into the fruit and cheese salad and toss gently to coat. Taste to correct seasonings. Refrigerate, covered, to chill.

4.   Just before serving, add 6 tablespoons of the pine nuts and toss again. Line the pitas with the chicory leaves and fill with the fruit and cheese salad. Sprinkle with the remaining toasted pine nuts.

Makes about 4 cups.

Variations   In place of the grapes and apple, substitute equal amounts of any of the following fruits or use a combination of several of them: pineapples, pears, fresh or dried figs, papayas, mangoes, and peaches.

SESAME-TOSSED PEAR WALDORF AND CHEESE

The Waldorf Astoria Hotel in New York where the apple version of the Waldorf salad originated might not recognize this one, but it surely is a winner! The subtle flavor of pear fairly screams for the piquant blue-cheese crumbles and the distinctive flavor of the ginger. And the Tahini-honey dressing melds everything together into a scrumptious salad.

½ cup raisins
3 cups peeled and diced pears
1 cup chopped celery
⅔ cup chopped walnuts or pecans
½ teaspoon ground ginger
¼ cup mayonnaise
¼ cup Tahini, (sesame seed paste), page 41
2 tablespoons toasted sesame seeds, page 165
1 tablespoon fresh lemon juice
1 teaspoon honey
½ cup crumbled blue cheese, or more to taste
Small Whole-Wheat Sesame Pitas, page 24, with the tops cut off
Whole walnuts or pecans (garnish)

1. Soak the raisins in boiling water until they are plumped, about 5 to 10 minutes. Drain thoroughly and dry with paper towels.

2. Combine the pears, celery, nuts, raisins, and ginger in a large bowl.

3. Whisk together the mayonnaise, tahini, sesame seeds, lemon juice, and honey in a small bowl.

4. Fold the dressing into the fruit salad and toss gently to coat. Sprinkle with the blue cheese and toss again to mix. Taste to correct seasonings. Refrigerate, covered, to chill.

5. Spoon the salad into the pitas. Garnish with whole walnuts or pecans.

Makes about 5 cups.

CARROT AND BANANA CURRY

With Cashew-Raisin Chutney

This enticingly simple vegetable-fruit curry is perfect for a pita pocket. It is essentially a carrot and banana toss, seasoned with the traditional spices so characteristically associated with this Indian dish. The yogurt imparts an important tanginess and a creamy light coating to carry the flavors of the spices.

¼ cup vegetable oil
½ teaspoon turmeric
½ teaspoon ground cumin
1 tablespoon peeled and slivered fresh ginger
½ teaspoon ground cardamom
¼ teaspoon caraway seeds
2 cups ripe, firm bananas, cut in ½-inch pieces
¾ pound carrots, peeled and cut in ¼-inch diagonal slices
Salt, to taste
Crushed red pepper flakes, to taste
1 teaspoon Madras curry powder
½ cup fresh orange juice
Dash of fresh lemon juice, or to taste
1 cup yogurt, preferably homemade, page 32
Small Whole-Wheat Honey Pitas, page 23, with the tops cut off
Shredded iceberg lettuce
Cashew-Raisin Chutney (recipe follows)

1. Heat the oil in a large skillet. Add the turmeric, cumin, ginger, cardamom, and caraway seeds and cook over low heat until fragrant, 2 to 3 minutes; be careful not to burn the spices.

ABOUT CURRIES IN A PITA

While curries are generally served on a bed of rice to absorb the sauce, these recipes include just enough sauce to bind the meat and vegetables together. Anything more moist will soak through the pocket. If, however, the curries seem to need more liquid as they cook, add a bit more of the liquid called for in the recipe (such as orange juice or chicken stock)—just enough to keep them moist while retaining the binding quality. As an extra precaution I have lined the pita pockets with shredded spinach or lettuce. For curry devotees, these pita stuffings laced with raitas and chutneys add new interest to a favorite dish. A note of warning, all the chutneys included here are *very* spicy—use them sparingly.

2. Add the bananas, carrots, salt, and red pepper flakes to the spices. Stir gently until thoroughly mixed, cover and sauté, stirring occasionally to keep the bananas and carrots from sticking, about 5 minutes.

3. Add the curry powder, orange juice, and lemon juice and stir gently. Be careful not to mash the bananas. Add the yogurt, cover and continue to simmer, stirring occasionally, until the curry is almost dry, 8 to 10 minutes. Taste to correct seasonings.

4. Line the pitas with the shredded lettuce. Spoon in the curry mixture and top with Cashew-Raisin Chutney.

Makes 4 to 6 servings.

Cashew-Raisin Chutney

1 cup raw cashews
2 hot green chiles, stemmed, seeded
*   and chopped*
¼ cup chopped fresh parsley
3 tablespoons fresh lemon juice
2 tablespoons peeled and chopped
*   fresh ginger*
1 tablespoon golden raisins
Dash of salt

Combine all the ingredients in a blender or food processor fitted with the metal blade. Process, until smooth, about 2 minutes. Add a little water, if necessary, to make a smooth paste. Refrigerate, covered, to chill. This fresh chutney is usually made to be used the same day but may be stored in the refrigerator for up to 1 week.

Makes about 1 cup.

Indian-Inspired Buffet Lunch

Chilled Cucumber and Yogurt
    Soup with Garlic Pita Crisps
Lamb, Apple, and Almond
    Curry with Mint Chutney in
    Wheat-Germ Honey Pitas
Curry Condiments: Cucumber
    Raita, sliced pimientoes,
    shredded coconut, toasted
    almonds
Carrot, Orange and Radish
    Salad
Flaming Apricot Walnut Rolls
Iced Spiced Anise Tea
Lemonade with orange-
    blossom Water

OVEN-BAKED CHICKEN TANDOORI

With Cucumber Raita and Coconut-Apple Chutney

Recall the last time you had chicken tandoori in an Indian restaurant. It was moist, tangy, and a pinkish-red after having been marinated in a peppery yogurt sauce and slowly baked in a special oven. While we don't have these special ovens at home, this Oven-Baked Chicken Tandoori comes very close to the real thing. Marinate the chicken nuggets for 24 hours so the flavors of the yogurt, lemon, coriander, anise, and crushed red pepper have plenty of time to tenderize and season the meat, and use the remaining marinade to baste these morsels while they bake.

2 cups yogurt, preferably homemade, page 32
2 tablespoons fresh lemon juice
1 tablespoon ground coriander
½ teaspoon crushed anise seed
½ teaspoon crushed red pepper flakes
Dash of salt, or to taste
3 pounds skinless, boneless chicken breasts, cut in 2-inch strips
⅓ cup vegetable oil
Small Basic Pitas, page 21, with the tops cut off
Shredded escarole
Cucumber Raita (recipe follows)
Coconut-Apple Chutney (recipe follows)

1.   One day before serving, combine the yogurt, lemon juice, coriander, anise, red pepper flakes, and salt in a large bowl.

2.   Add the chicken strips and toss to coat thoroughly. Cover and marinate in the refrigerator, turning the pieces occasionally, overnight or preferably for 24 hours.

3.   Preheat the oven to 375°F. Brush 3 tablespoons of vegetable oil over the bottom of a baking pan.

4.   Drain the chicken, reserving the marinade. Spread the chicken strips in the baking pan and brush them with the remaining oil.

5.   Bake the chicken, turning basting frequently with the reserved marinade, until tender, 30 to 40 minutes.

6.   Line the pitas with the shredded escarole and lightly lace with the cucumber raita. Spoon in the chicken and top with a little coconut-apple chutney.

Makes 6 to 8 servings.

Cucumber Raita

2 cucumbers, peeled, seeded, and shredded
Salt
2 cups yogurt, preferably homemade, page 32
4 scallions, finely chopped
¼ teaspoon ground cumin
Dash of cayenne, optional

1. Place the shredded cucumbers in a colander set over a medium bowl. Sprinkle lightly with salt and toss to mix. Set aside for 30 minutes. Squeeze out the water. Pat the cucumbers dry on paper towels.

2. Combine the remaining ingredients in a medium bowl. Add the cucumber and stir gently to blend. Taste to correct seasonings. Refrigerate, covered, to chill.

Makes about 3 cups.

Coconut-Apple Chutney

1 pound (about 3) green apples,
*   peeled and finely chopped*
Dash of salt
1 tablespoon fresh lemon juice
1 cup (8 ounces) packaged shredded
*   coconut (see note)*
3 medium onions, chopped
1 red or green bell pepper, cored,
*   seeded, and chopped*
1 tablespoon peeled and chopped
*   fresh ginger*

1. Place the apples in a medium bowl. Sprinkle lightly with the salt and lemon juice and toss to coat. Set aside to drain, about 10 minutes.

2. Place the onions, pepper, and ginger in a blender or food processor fitted with the metal blade, and process until finely chopped.

3. Drain the apples. Add the onion mixture and the coconut. Toss to mix thoroughly. Refrigerate, covered, to chill. This fresh chutney is usually made to be used the same day but may be stored in the refrigerator for up to 3 days.

Makes about 2½ cups.

Note: If you use fresh coconut, shred it in a food processor and add 2 teaspoons sugar.

Working With Hot Chiles

Always wear rubber gloves when you are working with hot chiles. Never rub your hands against your eyes, nose, or mouth because the tissue in these areas is extremely sensitive to the chile oils and fumes. After working with chiles, thoroughly wash both your hands and your gloves with soap and water.

CURRIED CRAB ROLLS
With Watercress Raita and Ginger-Raisin Chutney

Very similar to an Indian *Macchi Kofta* or a fish kebab, these crab rolls are fried to a crispy brown and served as appetizers or in pita pockets mounded with shredded lettuce and laced with Watercress Raita and Ginger-Raisin Chutney. Fresh cilantro, curry powder, and cayenne promise a characteristic Indian flavor.

3 cups shelled cooked crabmeat
3 eggs
3 tablespoons mayonnaise
1 cup fresh bread crumbs (about 2 slices of bread, crumbled)
1¼ cups flour
1 tablespoon finely chopped fresh cilantro
1 teaspoon Madras curry powder or more, to taste
Cayenne, to taste
¼ cup water
1 cup flour
1½ teaspoons salt
½ teaspoon pepper
Vegetable oil for frying
Small Sesame Pitas, page 22, with the tops cut off
Shredded Bibb lettuce
Watercress Raita (recipe follows)
Ginger-Raisin Chutney (recipe follows)

1. Flake the crabmeat and place in a medium bowl. Beat 2 of the eggs until frothy and add to the crabmeat. Add the bread crumbs, cilantro, curry powder, and cayenne. Toss to combine thoroughly. Shape the crabmeat into 8 rolls; set aside.

2. Beat the remaining egg with the water in a small bowl. Combine the flour, salt, and pepper in a pie plate.

Dip the crabmeat rolls first in the beaten egg, then roll in the seasoned flour, coating well. Place on a wax-paper lined plate and refrigerate, covered, until the rolls are firm and the coating is set, about 1 hour.

3. Pour the oil to a depth of ½ inch in a deep skillet and heat until hot but not smoking. Fry the crab rolls, turning frequently, until golden brown, about 3 to 5 minutes. Drain on paper towels.

4. Line the pitas with the shredded lettuce and lace with the watercress raita. Put a crab roll inside each pocket and top with a little ginger-raisin chutney.

Makes 4 servings or 8 rolls.

Watercress Raita

2 cups yogurt, preferably homemade, page 32
1 cup finely chopped watercress
1 clove garlic, crushed
1 tablespoon finely chopped green bell pepper
¼ teaspoon ground cumin
Salt, to taste
Cayenne, to taste

Combine all the ingredients in a medium bowl. Stir them gently to blend. Taste to correct seasonings. Refrigerate, covered, to chill.

Makes 3 cups.

Ginger-Raisin Chutney

1½ cups peeled and chopped fresh
* ginger*
1 hot green chile, stemmed, seeded,
* and chopped*
3 tablespoons red wine vinegar
2 tablespoons golden raisins
Dash of salt

Combine all the ingredients in a blender or food processor fitted with the metal blade. Process until smooth, about 2 minutes. Add a little water if necessary, to make a smooth paste. Refrigerate, covered, to chill. This fresh chutney is usually made to be used the same day but may be stored in the refrigerator for up to 1 week.

Makes about 1 cup.

LAMB, APPLE, AND ALMOND CURRY
With Mint Chutney

The last-minute addition of yogurt blends with the tomato paste to impart an added zest and create a pinkish sauce to coat this lamb, apple, and almond combo. Shredded spinach and mint chutney add a crowning touch!

3 tablespoons vegetable oil or more,
* if necessary*
2 pounds lamb leg or shoulder, cut
* in 1-inch cubes*
1 large onion, chopped
2 cloves garlic, crushed
2 tablespoons chopped fresh
* cilantro*
1 tablespoon peeled and slivered
* fresh ginger*
1 tablespoon Madras curry powder
1 tablespoon ground cumin
1 tablespoon tomato paste
2 tablespoons flour
Salt and freshly ground black
* pepper, to taste*

1½ to 2 cups hot chicken stock
2 medium green apples, peeled and
* chopped*
½ cup slivered almonds
¾ cup yogurt, preferably
* homemade, page 32*
Small Wheat-Germ Honey Pitas,
* page 24, with the tops cut off*
Shredded fresh spinach
Mint Chutney (recipe follows)

1. Heat the oil in a large skillet. Working in batches, add the lamb and sauté over medium-high heat, turning often, until well browned, about 15 minutes. Using a slotted spoon, remove the lamb as it is browned from the skillet and place in a bowl.

2. Reduce the heat to medium and add the onion and garlic to the skillet and sauté, stirring frequently, about 5 minutes; add more oil, if necessary.

3. Add the cilantro, ginger, curry powder, cumin, tomato paste, flour, and salt and pepper, and cook over low heat, stirring constantly, until the spices become fragrant, about 1 minute; take care not to burn them.

4. Return the lamb to the skillet. Add the chicken stock beginning with 1½ cups and increasing to 2 cups, if necessary. (You need enough liquid to cook the meat yet not so much that it will drip through a pita pocket. Cover and cook over low heat, stirring occasionally, until the lamb is tender, about 1 hour.

5. Add the apples and almonds and cook until the apples are soft, about 5 minutes.

6. Just before serving, stir in the yogurt. Heat thoroughly, stirring constantly.

7. Line the pitas with the shredded spinach. Spoon in the lamb curry and top with mint chutney.

Makes 6 to 8 servings.

Mint Chutney

2 cups packed fresh mint leaves
3 scallions, chopped
1 hot green chile, stemmed, seeded
*   and chopped*
3 tablespoons fresh lemon juice
2 tablespoons peeled and chopped
*   fresh ginger*
1 teaspoon sugar, or more, to taste
Dash of salt

Combine all the ingredients in a blender or food processor fitted with the metal blade. Process until smooth, about 2 minutes. Add a little water, if necessary, to make a smooth paste. Refrigerate, covered, to chill. This fresh chutney is usually made to be used the same day but may be stored in the refrigerator for up to 1 week.

Makes about 1 cup.

PITA BURRITOS

I remember eating the best burritos ever at one of the many Mexican stands at Farmer's Market in Los Angeles. I thought then about making a Mediterranean-style burrito by rolling ''refried'' garbanzo beans (instead of refried pink or pinto beans) in a pita seasoned with scallions and garlic and topped with melted cheese. If you've any leftover *Hummus Bi Tahini*, use that instead of the garbanzos.

6 Griddle-Baked Pitas, page 31
¼ cup olive oil, or more, if
    necessary
¾ cup dried chickpeas (garbanzo
    beans), cooked and drained (see
    page 40) or 2 cups (1 pound can)
    chickpeas, drained and rinsed
2 cloves garlic, crushed
Salt and freshly ground black
    pepper, to taste
¼ cup finely chopped fresh cilantro
5 scallions, chopped
1 cup grated Monterey Jack
Harissa (hot pepper sauce), page
    108

1. Stack the pitas on a large square of aluminum foil. Seal and set aside.

2. Heat the oil in a large skillet. Add the beans and sauté over medium heat, mashing and stirring, to make a soft spreadable paste. Add more oil and some water, if necessary. Add the garlic, salt, and pepper, and stir until the mixture is softened and heated throughout. Taste to correct seasonings.

3. Preheat the oven to 300°F. As the oven is preheating, place the foil-wrapped pitas in the oven, until warm and pliable, 5 to 8 minutes. Remove from the oven and unwrap. Lightly grease a large baking dish.

4. Spoon ⅓ cup of the seasoned bean mixture in the center of each pita, spreading it to within 1 inch of the edge. Top the bean mixture with the cilantro, scallions, and cheese, dividing it evenly among the 6 pitas. Roll the pitas closed and secure each with a toothpick. Place, folded-side down, in the prepared baking dish.

5. Bake in the oven until the cheese melts and the mixture is hot, 10 to 15 minutes.

6. Serve each burrito in a square of parchment paper and lace generously with *harissa*.

Makes 6 burritos.

CRISPY SESAME CHICKEN STRIPS

Friends will devour these tender oven-baked strips of sesame-seeded chicken stuffed in pitas and topped with Carrot, Orange, and Radish Salad.

1 egg
¼ cup water
1 cup dry bread crumbs
2 tablespoons flour
2 tablespoons toasted sesame seeds
Salt and freshly ground black pepper, to taste
Dash of cayenne, to taste
2 whole (about 1½ pounds) skinless, boneless chicken breasts, pounded and cut into 3-inch strips
½ cup vegetable oil
Sesame Pitas, page 22, cut into halves
Shredded red leaf lettuce
Carrot, Orange, and Radish Salad, page 94
Sesame-Honey Sauce, page 152

1. Beat the egg and water in a small bowl. Combine the bread crumbs, flour, sesame seeds, salt, pepper, and cayenne in a pie plate. Dip the chicken strips first in the beaten egg, then roll in the bread crumbs, coating well. Place on a wax-paper-lined plate and refrigerate to set the coating, about 30 minutes to 1 hour.

2. Pour the oil into a baking pan and place in the oven. Preheat the oven to 375°F. Remove the baking pan from the oven. Add the chicken strips and coat them evenly with the oil.

3. Place the chicken in the oven and bake, turning occasionally to brown all the sides, until golden-brown and tender, 35 to 40 minutes. Be careful not to overcook as the chicken will dry out.

4. Line the pitas with the shredded lettuce and fill them with the chicken strips. Top with Carrot, Orange, and Radish Salad and lace with Sesame-Honey Sauce.

Makes 4 to 6 servings.

PITA STROGANOFF

Mix sautéed onion, garlic, and mushrooms with lamb, season it delicately with sherry, then stir in tangy yogurt for a hearty Stroganoff.

3 tablespoons butter
1 large onion, chopped
1 clove garlic, minced
½ pound mushrooms, wiped clean
*   with damp paper towels, and*
*   sliced*
1½ pounds lean lamb, cut in thin
*   1-inch strips*
¾ to 1 cup water
¼ cup dry sherry
Salt and freshly ground black
*   pepper, to taste*
1 tablespoon flour
1 cup yogurt, preferably
*   homemade, page 32*
Small Wheat-Germ Honey Pitas,
*   page 24, with the tops cut off*
Shredded Bibb lettuce
Chopped tomatoes (garnish)
Chopped parsley (garnish)

1. Melt the butter in a large skillet. Add the onion, garlic, and mushrooms, and sauté over medium heat until all the water has evaporated from the mushrooms and the onions are soft but not brown, 5 minutes.

2. Stir in the lamb and cook, stirring occasionally, until the meat loses its pink color, about 5 minutes.

3. Add the water, sherry, salt, and pepper. Stir and cover. Reduce the heat to low and continue cooking, stirring occasionally, until tender, about 45 minutes to 1 hour.

4. In a small bowl, blend the flour with the yogurt. Slowly stir it into the meat mixture. Continue cooking, stirring constantly, until the sauce is heated through and thickened. Taste to correct seasonings.

5. Line the pitas with the shredded lettuce and fill with the stroganoff. Top each with the chopped tomatoes and parsley.

Makes 4 to 6 servings.

THE PITA CROQUE MONSIEUR

Make a French sandwich by spreading the insides of a Basic Pita with Dijon-style mustard and filling it with thin slices of ham and cheese—Swiss, Gruyère, or muenster. Carefully dip it in a mixture of egg and milk (1 tablespoon milk to 1 egg) and sauté it in a blend of 1 tablespoon butter and 1 tablespoon vegetable oil, as you would French Toast. Serve it with a light cheese sauce for extra zest.

MUSTARD STEAK AND BUCHERON

If you think the only way to cook flank steak is to braise it, I beg you to try it broiled. When we were first married, my husband introduced me to this way of cooking and slicing this normally less tender cut of beef. Its tenderness lies in the slicing. Slather it first with Dijon-style mustard and Worcestershire sauce, broil it to your favorite doneness—I like it medium-rare—then diagonally slice it paper-thin. Pile it in a pita topped with a mild goat cheese, chopped scallions, and tomatoes. You've a memorable sandwich offering that calls for a mug of beer to top it off!

¼ cup Dijon-style mustard
2 tablespoons Worcestershire sauce
1 pound flank steak
¼ cup butter, softened
Small Basic Pitas, page 21, with the tops cut off
Freshly ground black pepper
8 ounces Bucheron or similar soft goat cheese
Arugula (garnish)
Chopped scallions (garnish)
Chopped tomatoes (garnish)
Salt and freshly ground black pepper, to taste

1. Blend the mustard and Worcestershire sauce in a small cup. Slather both sides of flank steak with the mustard mixture. Cover and marinate in the refrigerator, turning occasionally, 1 hour or more.

2. Butter the insides of the pitas and wrap in clean, dry towels to prevent them from drying out. Set aside.

3. Preheat the broiler.

4. Sprinkle the steak on both sides with the freshly ground black pepper. Broil to medium-rare, about 5 minutes on each side.

5. Cut the steak on the diagonal into very thin slices and divide it and the Bucheron evenly among the buttered pitas. Garnish with the arugula, chopped scallions, and tomatoes. Season with salt and pepper to taste.

Makes 4 servings.

Super-Bowl Supper

Fried Lemon-Laced Cheese in Griddle-Baked Pitas
Piquant Pickled Turnips
Pita Charcuterie
Mustard Steak and Bucheron in Basic Pitas
Tomato and Onion Salad
Minted Potato Salad
Stuffed Dates in Pita wedges
Iced Beer
Hot Coffee

GINGERED TOFU AND VEGETABLE TOSS

The zippy flavor of ginger and the subtlety of tofu join forces to create these wonderful crispy-tender golden brown nuggets of goodness! Shredded Chinese cabbage and Coconut-Apple Chutney make great companions.

2 tablespoons vegetable oil
4 scallions, chopped
1 clove garlic, minced
Crushed red pepper flakes, to taste
1 cake (about 4 ounces) tofu, cut into 1-inch cubes
1 small cucumber, peeled, cut in half lengthwise, seeded and sliced
½ pound bean sprouts
1 teaspoon peeled and slivered fresh ginger
½ pound snow peas, trimmed
1 tablespoon soy sauce, or more, to taste
Medium Whole-Wheat Sesame Pitas, page 24, cut into halves
Shredded Chinese cabbage
Coconut-Apple Chutney, page 135

1. Heat the oil in a large skillet or wok. Add the scallions and garlic and stir-fry over medium-high heat, about 1 minute. Stir in the crushed red pepper flakes and continue cooking to release the flavor, about 10 seconds.

2. Add the tofu and stir-fry for 2 minutes. Add the cucumber, bean sprouts, and ginger and continue cooking until well coated and hot, about 1 to 2 minutes.

3. Add the snow peas and soy sauce and stir-fry 1 minute longer. Taste to correct seasonings.

4. Line the pitas with the shredded cabbage and fill with the tofu-vegetable toss. Add a dollop of coconut-apple chutney on top.

Makes 4 to 6 servings.

PEACEMAKER IN A POCKET

Peacemaker is the term given to a well-known New Orleans tradition. Years ago, errant husbands coming home late at night would bring hot, crispy oyster-filled loaves known as Les Mediatrices or mediators to appease their waiting wives. I've adapted the recipe to stuff the succulent oysters in pita pockets instead of hollowing out French loaves.

Flour, for coating
2 eggs
¼ cup water
Dry bread crumbs
3 dozen fresh-shucked oysters or 2
    cans (7 ounces each) frozen
    oysters, thawed
¼ cup melted butter (1 tablespoon
    per loaf)
4 medium Basic Pitas, page 21, cut
    into halves
Vegetable oil, for frying
Fresh lemon juice (garnish)

1. Place the flour on a large plate. Beat the eggs and water in a small bowl. Place the bread crumbs on a second plate. Drain the oysters, then coat them with flour, dip them in the beaten eggs, and roll in the bread crumbs, coating well. Place on a wax-paper-lined plate and refrigerate, covered, to set the coating, about 30 minutes to 1 hour.

2. Butter the inside of the pitas and stack on a large square of aluminum foil. Seal and set aside.

3. Preheat the oven to 300°F.

4. Pour the oil to a depth of ½ inch in a deep skillet and heat until hot but not smoking. Working in batches, add the oysters a few at a time, and fry them over medium-high heat until golden, about 3 to 4 minutes; do not crowd the skillet. Drain the oysters on paper towels.

5. Warm the pitas in the oven for 2 to 3 minutes. Be careful that they do not get too crisp.

6. Fill the warm pita halves with hot oysters. Drizzle with lemon juice and serve immediately.

Makes 4 servings.

Orangeade with Orange-Blossom Water

A first cousin to lemonade, serve this hot or cold.

1½ cups fresh orange juice
¼ cup fresh lemon juice
¼ cup ice water
½ to 1 teaspoon orange-
    blossom water, to taste
Sugar, to taste
Ice
Orange slices (garnish)
Fresh basil leaves (garnish)

Combine the orange juice, lemon juice, ice water, orange-blossom water, and sugar in a pitcher. Blend well. Pour into ice-filled glasses. Garnish with orange slices and basil leaves.

Makes 2 to 3 servings.

ORANGE-GINGERED CHICKEN

Orange and ginger combine wonderfully with chicken in this tasty stir-fry with vegetables all piled into Poppy-Seed Pitas.

½ cup fresh orange juice
2 tablespoons soy sauce
1 teaspoon cornstarch
½ teaspoon ground ginger
3 tablespoons fresh ginger, peeled and cut into julienne strips
½ teaspoon crushed red pepper flakes, optional
2 cloves garlic, crushed
1 pound skinless, boneless chicken breasts, cut into julienne strips
2 tablespoons vegetable oil
10 ounces fresh or frozen snow peas, trimmed and cut into strips
1 small red bell pepper, cored, seeded, and cut into bite-size pieces
½ pound mushrooms, wiped clean with damp paper towels, and sliced
Medium Poppy-Seed Pitas, page 22, cut into halves
2 cups shredded Chinese cabbage
Chopped fresh cilantro (garnish)

1. Combine the orange juice, soy sauce, cornstarch, ground and fresh ginger, red pepper flakes, and garlic in a large bowl. Add the chicken and stir to coat. Cover and marinate in the refrigerator, turning the pieces occasionally, about 2 hours.

2. Drain the chicken and reserve the marinade. Heat the oil in a large skillet or wok. Add the chicken and stir-fry over medium-high heat until cooked, about 5 to 8 minutes. Add the snow peas, bell pepper, and mushrooms, and continue cooking, tossing frequently until the vegetables are crisp-tender, about 3 to 5 minutes. Add the reserved marinade and cook until the liquid has been reduced by half.

3. Line the pitas with the shredded cabbage, fill with the chicken-vegetable mixture, and top with the cilantro.

Makes 4 to 6 servings.

PITA SWEETS

Pitas work most creatively when it comes to desserts. Turn them into crêpes, puffs, rolls, puddings, and crisps to be combined with fresh and dried fruits, nuts, soft cheeses, and many other classic ingredients of the Middle East which are popular today as healthy alternatives to calorie-laden tortes and rich chocolate cakes.

Pita is also a handy accompaniment to simple sweets such as Stuffed Dates, Pressed Apricot Rolls, and Halvah, and Sweet Pita Crisps are delicious with light flavorful dips such as Sesame and Carob Sauce. Whatever your choices from the pita variations on old-fashioned American favorites such as Spiced Apple Pudding with Vanilla Sauce to exotic Flaming Apricot Walnut Rolls, guests will compliment your ingenuity and ask for more.

PITA CHEESE CRÊPES
With Orange-Blossom Syrup

Almost every country in the world has a cheese-filled pastry and the Middle East is no exception. In fact, there are numerous varieties—some rolled in phyllo pastry, others in a pancake-like crêpe and still others in a wheat- or farina-topped confection, but the common denominator is that they are all laced with a wonderful syrup of sugar, lemon juice, and orange-blossom water. This recipe uses the paper-thin but chewy Griddle-Baked Pitas to wrap around sweetened Yogurt Cheese or ricotta cheese. An exotic way to end a dinner for special guests. Serve them with Turkish coffee.

1½ cups unsalted Yogurt Cheese, page 33, or ricotta cheese
2 tablespoons sugar, or more to taste
1 tablespoon grated lemon rind
6 Griddle-baked Pitas (7–8 inches), page 31
2 tablespoons melted butter
1½ cups Orange-Blossom Syrup (recipe follows)

1. Blend the yogurt cheese or ricotta with the sugar and grated lemon rind until smooth. Taste to correct seasonings. Set aside.

2. Cut the pitas in half and square the edges to make 12 strips, 3½ to 4 inches wide.

3. Preheat the oven to 350°F. Lightly grease a shallow 1½-quart baking dish.

4. Divide the cheese mixture equally between the pita strips, spreading it to the edges. Roll the strips lengthwise and place, seam-side down, in the baking dish. Brush with the melted butter.

5. Bake, until heated through, 15 to 20 minutes. Serve warm, topped with orange-blossom syrup.

Makes 12 crêpes or 6 servings.

Orange-Blossom Syrup

3 cups sugar
1½ cups water
1 tablespoon fresh lemon juice
1 teaspoon orange-blossom water, or more, to taste

1. Combine the sugar, water, and lemon juice in a medium saucepan. Bring to a boil over high heat, stirring frequently. Reduce the heat to low and cook, uncovered, until the syrup falls in two or three heavy drops from a spoon, or registers 212°F on a candy thermometer.

2. Immediately remove from the heat and let cool. Stir in the orange-blossom water. Serve the syrup at room temperature.

Makes about 2 cups.

Variations *Rose Water Syrup* Substitute ½ teaspoon rose water, or more, if desired, for the orange-blossom water.

Cinnamon Syrup: Add 1 cinnamon stick to the syrup after reducing the heat to low. Omit the orange-blossom water.

FLAMING APRICOT-WALNUT ROLLS

The tangy flavor of apricots is enhanced immeasurably when these elegant little rolls are laced with Cognac and flambéed. They make a nice change of pace from Crêpes Suzettes.

½ pound dried apricots
½ cup sugar
1 tablespoon fresh lemon juice
½ teaspoon grated orange rind, or more to taste
½ cup chopped walnuts
6 Griddle-baked Pitas (7–8 inches), page 31
1½ cups unsalted Yogurt Cheese, page 33
2 tablespoons melted butter
1½ cups Rose Water Syrup, page 148
¼ cup Cognac

1. One day before serving, put the apricots in a medium bowl and cover with cold water. Let them soak overnight. Drain, reserving the water and cut the apricots into small pieces.

2. Place the reserved apricot water in a saucepan. Add the sugar and lemon juice and bring to a boil. Boil for 5 minutes. Add the apricots, reduce the heat, and simmer, stirring frequently, until the liquid has thickened, 30 to 45 minutes. Add the orange rind and nuts and cook for another 5 minutes. Remove from the heat and let cool.

3. Cut the pitas in half and square the edges to make 12 strips, 3½ to 4 inches wide.

4. Preheat the oven to 350°F. Lightly grease a shallow 1½-quart baking dish.

5. Divide the yogurt cheese equally between the pita strips, spreading it to the edges. Spread a layer of the glazed apricots over the cheese. Tightly roll the strips lengthwise and secure them with toothpicks. Place, seam-side down, in the baking dish. Brush with the melted butter.

6. Bake until heated through, 15 to 20 minutes. Transfer the warm apricot rolls to a chafing dish and pour the Rose Water Syrup over them.

7. Just before serving, heat the Cognac in a small saucepan over medium heat and pour it immediately over the rolls. Carefully ignite the Cognac and let the flames go out. Serve the rolls with a generous measure of the Cognac-laced syrup, about ¼ cup per serving.

Makes 12 rolls or 6 servings.

SPICED GLAZED FIGS WITH HAZELNUTS

A little of these spicy figs with a toasted pita crisp is heavenly with a cup of demitasse. Or serve them as a confection for a lazy weekend brunch.

1 pound dried Calimyrna figs, chopped
Fresh orange juice, to cover (about 3 cups)
½ cup sugar
Dash of nutmeg
Dash of ginger
¼ teaspoon ground cinnamon
¾ cup chopped walnuts
1 tablespoon fresh lemon juice
Sweet Sesame Pita Crisps, page 28

1. Place the figs in a medium saucepan. Add the orange juice just to cover and let soak for about 30 minutes.

2. Cook over medium heat for 30 minutes. Add the sugar, nutmeg, ginger, and cinnamon. Reduce the heat and continue cooking until the figs are glazed and mixture is slightly thickened, about 15 to 20 minutes.

3. Remove from the heat and add the walnuts and lemon juice. Serve warm or cold with sweet sesame pita crisps.

Makes about 6 servings.

Variation *Glazed Apricots with Walnuts:* Substitute dried apricots for the figs; cook as above, omitting spices.

Tip: You may stew and glaze whole figs and apricots instead of chopping them, if desired.

STUFFED DATES IN PITA WEDGES

Stuffed dates in pita wedges are excellent served with wine and cheese or as a light dessert. Make a batch and give them to a special friend, with a package of pita, of course. Pit large dates or use pitted dates. Slit them enough to insert walnut pieces, pecan halves, or blanched salted almonds. Or, stuff them with unsalted Yogurt Cheese, page 33. Press the edges of the dates together to anchor the stuffing and shake the dates in a paper bag filled with a mixture of brown sugar and cinnamon. Serve them inside Basic Pita wedges.

TURKISH COFFEE
(Kahwe Turki)

Kahwe, meaning coffee, plays an important role in Middle-Eastern life. An unsweetened version is always served during a sad occasion while a sweet blend is enjoyed at celebrations and other happy times. Many a business deal has also been sealed over a foamy cup of demitasse. The foaminess is the secret to a good cup of Turkish coffee. Methodically follow the steps outlined below and you will make a perfect pot every time.

6 demitasse cups cold water
6 heaping teaspoons pulverized Turkish Coffee
Sugar, to taste (optional)

Pour the water into a saucepan or tapered, long-handled brass or porcelain Turkish coffee pot. Bring to a boil and add sugar, if desired. Gradually add the coffee, stirring constantly, until it returns to a boil and becomes foamy. Remove from the heat and let the froth recede in the coffee pot. Return to the heat and bring the coffee back to a boil, stirring occasionally to keep the coffee foamy. Repeat this procedure once more. Spoon a portion of the foam into each demitasse cup and pour in the coffee. The foam will rise to the top.

Makes about 6 demitasse servings.

Variations *Cardamom Coffee:*   Add 2 to 3 split cardamom pods to the coffee before you add it to the water.

Spiced Coffee: Add 1 teaspoon of ground cinnamon or ginger to the coffee before you add it to the water.

BAKED RUBY QUINCE WITH WALNUTS

I remember mother serving juicy chunks of preserved sweet quince topped with walnuts—they were always so good but ever too sweet. This recipe brings to mind those ruby red preserves—the quince turn a reddish color as they cook—without all that sugar and calorie-laden guilt! Try it served with crisp pita wedges for your next Sunday brunch or lazy weekend breakfast. According to legend, the early Greeks and Romans considered the quince sacred to the Goddess of Love. If you gave a quince to the one you love it was tantamount to an engagement symbol.

4 ripe, bright-yellow quince, peeled, cored, and cut in quarters
½ cup sugar
2 cups apple juice
1 tablespoon fresh lemon juice
1 teaspoon rose water (optional)
Chopped walnuts
Yogurt, preferably homemade, page 32
Cinnamon Pita Crisps, page 28

1. Preheat the oven to 300°F.

2. Place the quince quarters in a 1½-quart baking dish. Sprinkle with the sugar and add the apple juice. It should come to a depth of ½-inch in the baking dish (use more or less as needed).

3. Bake, basting occasionally with the syrup, until tender, glazed and reddish in color, 2 hours. Remove from the oven and add the lemon juice and rose water, if desired. Cool to room temperature.

4. Serve topped with chopped walnuts and a dollup of yogurt, and accompanied by cinnamon pita crisps.

Makes 4 servings.

Sweet Pita Crisps With Dipping Sauces

The best desserts are sometimes those that require very little work. This one fits the bill. Try it for a sweet ending to a casual weekend supper. Prepare 3 bowls each with ½ cup Tahini (sesame seed paste), page 41. Stir in ½ cup honey to the first bowl, ½ cup carob syrup to the second bowl, and ½ cup maple syrup to the third bowl to make each sauce. Add a little water if you prefer a thinner sauce. Serve with Sweet Sesame Pita Crisps, page 28, surrounded by apple and pear slices which are also good dipped in the sauces.

SPICED APPLE PITA PUDDING
With Vanilla Sauce

This old-fashioned bread pudding topped with apples is a great way to use up the tops left over from pitas you have filled with sandwich fixings.

½ cup raisins
3 tablespoons butter
4 cups pita cubes, cut in 1½-inch pieces
3 eggs
1½ cups milk
½ cup heavy cream
⅔ cup sugar
½ teaspoon grated orange rind
½ teaspoon ground cinnamon
1 large Red Delicious apple, peeled, cored, and cut into ½-inch wedges
1½ to 2 cups Vanilla Sauce (recipe follows)

1. Soak the raisins in boiling water until they are plumped, about 10 to 15 minutes. Drain thoroughly and dry with paper towels.

2. Melt the butter in a large skillet. Add the pita cubes and sauté over medium heat, tossing lightly, until well coated and just beginning to brown, about 5 minutes. Put the bread cubes and any remaining butter into a lightly buttered 9 x 9-inch glass baking dish. Add the raisins to the bread cubes and mix together.

3. Combine the eggs, milk, cream, ½ cup of the sugar, and the orange rind in a medium bowl and beat together thoroughly. Pour over the bread cubes and raisin mixture, making certain the bread is thoroughly immersed. Refrigerate, covered with plastic wrap, for 1 hour.

4. Preheat the oven to 350°F.

5. Combine the remaining sugar with the cinnamon. Arrange the apple wedges on top of the pudding and sprinkle with the cinnamon-sugar mixture.

6. Place the baking dish in a large baking pan. Add enough hot water to come ⅔ of the way up the sides of the pan. Bake in the center of the oven, until a thin-bladed knife inserted 1 inch from the edge comes out clean, 40 to 45 minutes. Remove from the oven and let cool to room temperature.

Makes 6 to 8 servings.

Vanilla Sauce

⅓ cup sugar
1½ tablespoons cornstarch
¼ teaspoon salt
1⅔ cups boiling water
3 tablespoons butter, cut into small
* pieces*
2 teaspoons vanilla extract

1. Combine the sugar, cornstarch, and salt in a medium saucepan. Stir in the boiling water and cook over medium heat, stirring constantly, until thickened and clear, about 6 to 8 minutes. Simmer for an additional 3 minutes to cook the cornstarch.

2. Remove from the heat and add the butter and vanilla extract. Stir to blend. When the butter has melted, serve warm over the pudding.

Makes about 2 cups.

Pita Apple Crisps

Turn little pita loaves into a handy crust for a quickie Apple Crisp, a favorite among children and adults alike.

Slit small pitas into individual rounds, spread them with softened butter, and top with a hefty dollop of applesauce seasoned with sugar and cinnamon. Place them on a greased baking sheet and bake in a preheated 350°F oven until they are warm and heated through, about 10 to 12 minutes.

They are heavenly served warm and topped with a scoop of vanilla ice cream.

PITA AND HALVAH

Halvah is a confection made of ground sesame seeds and honey, sugar, or glucose, bound together with egg white. Originally a Turkish specialty, halvah is now widely found throughout the Middle East. It comes plain, marbled, chocolate-coated, or with pistachios and may be purchased in the refrigerated sections of well-stocked supermarkets, health food stores, gourmet delis, or in any Near or Middle Eastern grocery store. It is traditionally eaten with pita bread, which balances its cloyingly sweet taste.

Cut small pitas into halves or triangles and insert slices of halvah. Serve these with apple slices, grapes, or melon balls, and offer strong, sweet Turkish coffee to make a delightful ending to simple meal.

PISTACHIO AND BANANA TOFFEE ROLLS

With Grand Marnier Syrup and Crème Fraîche

These fruit and nut rolls laced with warm Grand Marnier Syrup and Crème Fraîche make an unusual dessert for a special occasion.

1½ cups coarsely chopped pistachio nuts
¼ cup firmly packed light brown sugar
2 tablespoons butter, softened
6 Griddle-Baked Pitas (7–8 inches), page 31
3 medium bananas, peeled and cut in half (each half should be about 2½ to 3 inches long)
2 tablespoons butter, melted
1½ cups Grand Marnier Syrup, (recipe follows)
Crème Fraîche (recipe follows)

1. Combine the nuts, sugar, and softened butter in a medium bowl. Set aside.

2. Cut the pitas in half and square the edges to make 12 strips, 3½ to 4 inches wide.

3. Preheat the oven to 350°F. Lightly grease a shallow 1½-quart baking dish.

4. Divide the nut mixture equally between the pita strips, spreading it to the edges. Top each strip with a banana half. Tightly roll the strips lengthwise and secure them with toothpicks. Place, seamside down, in the baking dish. Brush with the melted butter.

5. Bake until heated through, about 15 to 20 minutes. Serve warm drizzled with the Grand Marnier Syrup, about ¼ cup per serving. Top with a dollop of crème fraîche.

Makes 6 servings.

Grand Marnier Syrup

2 cups sugar
2 cups water
1 tablespoon fresh lemon juice
2 tablespoons Grand Marnier

1. Combine the sugar, water, and lemon juice in a medium saucepan. Bring to a boil over high heat, stirring frequently. Reduce the heat to low and cook, uncovered, until the syrup falls in two or three heavy drops from a spoon, or registers 212°F on a candy thermometer.

2. Immediately remove from the heat and let cool. Stir in the Grand Marnier. Serve the syrup at room temperature.

Makes 2 cups.

Crème Fraîche

½ cup heavy cream
½ cup sour cream

1. One day before serving, whisk together the heavy cream and sour cream in a medium bowl. Cover and set aside in a warm place until thickened, 8 hours to overnight.

2. Refrigerate, covered, to chill for 4 to 6 hours to develop its characteristic tart flavor.

Makes about 1 cup.

PRESSED APRICOT ROLLS

As children we used to call this candy-like confection made from puréed apricots "shoe leather" because it looked like the leather which was sold by the yard before it was made into shoes. When we purchased it we literally bought it by the yard and tore it into bite-size pieces to eat. Once only available as an import from the Middle-East, it is now processed and sold widely by American food companies or it can be made without too much fuss at home.

Grind 2 pounds of dried apricots and 1 pound of dried peaches twice in a food grinder using the finest cutting wheel or process them in a food processor fitted with the metal blade until they are puréed or finely minced. Sprinkle a cutting board heavily with confectioners' sugar and knead the apricot-peach mixture until it is smooth, about 8 to 10 minutes, then pat and roll it to a thickness of ⅛-inch. Cut it into 2-inch strips and roll each into a tight little roll. Set them overnight in an uncovered dish or pan to dry. Store in an airtight container for up to 3 weeks. Makes about 3 pounds.

These dainty rolls are a favorite lunch-box treat for children, or a convenient dessert served with Sesame Pita toast and a piquant cheese such as Roquefort or Kasseri.

GLAZED PITA PUFFS
(Awamat)

These syrup-bathed doughnut puffs are favorite sweetmeats all over Middle Eastern and Mediterranean countries. Called awamat in Arabic, zeppoli in Italy, diples in Greece, and doughnuts in America, these deep-fried dollops of dough are a little bite of heaven!

½ recipe Basic Pita dough, page 21, prepared through step 2
Vegetable oil, for frying
1½ to 2 cups Orange-Blossom Syrup, page 148

1. Place the dough in a large greased bowl and turn the dough over to bring the greased side up. Cover the bowl with a clean dry towel and let the dough rise in a warm draft-free area until it is light and spongy, about 1 to 1½ hours.

2. Pinch off pieces of the dough about 1 to 1½ inches in diameter. Shape into balls, cover with a clean dry towel and let them rise for another 30 minutes.

3. Pour the oil to a depth of 1½ inches in a deep skillet and heat until hot but not smoking. Working in batches of 5 or 6 at a time, fry the pieces until they are golden-brown on all sides, about 1 minute. Using a slotted spoon, remove them and drain on paper towels.

4. Dip the warm fritters into the cold syrup and place them on a serving platter. Drizzle more syrup over the puffs before serving.

Makes about 3 dozen.

Variations *Sugared Puffs:* Instead of dipping the puffs into the syrup, dust them lightly with confectioners' sugar.

MINT TEA
(Shī)

Shī, pronounced similarly all over the Middle East, even if spelled differently, means tea. This minty version is refreshing, especially when served with Glazed Pita Puffs, page 157, or Pita Apple Crisps, page 154. In the summer, pour the tea over ice and garnish it with a mint sprig and a slice of orange for a thirst-quenching cooler.

4 cups water
3 teaspoons green China tea, such as Gunpowder
Sugar or honey, to taste
⅔ cup fresh mint sprigs, chopped
Additional fresh mint sprigs (garnish)

Pour the water into a large saucepan and bring to a boil. Stir in the tea and sugar or honey. Place the mint sprigs in a warmed teapot and pour in the sweetened tea. Cover and let steep for 5 to 7 minutes. Strain into tea cups or glasses. Top each with a mint sprig.

Makes about 4 to 6 servings.

GLOSSARY
AND
INDEX

GLOSSARY

What follows is an explanation of various recipe ingredients that may be unfamiliar. If you have trouble finding bulgur, fava beans, Kasseri, Alphonse or Calamata olives, orange-blossom water, pine nuts, rose water, Salonika peppers, sesame seeds, sumac, tahini, or zahter these and other ingredients are all available by mail-order from the two fine establishments listed below.

Malko Importing Corporation
182 Atlantic Avenue
Brooklyn, NY 11201
(718) 624-2049

Eastern Star Bakery
440 SW Eighth Street
Miami, FL 33130
(305) 854-6381

Bulgur

A grain product made by parboiling and drying whole-wheat kernels, and crushing them into various sizes from fine to coarse grades. It is not to be confused with cracked wheat or crushed wheat. Bulgur is used for making *Kibbeh*, page 51, and *Tabbouleh*, page 98. It is available in health food stores and Middle Eastern groceries.

There seems to be a wide variety of opinion among food experts and cookbook writers on how to prepare bulgur. Some feel it should be soaked for long periods in hot water while others suggest cooking it first. None of this is necessary, in my opinion, as such methods will make the bulgur too soft and mushy. Simply rinse the bulgur and place it in a bowl. Cover with cool tap water and let soak until it is tender to the bite, about 20 to 30 minutes. Drain thoroughly and squeeze out any excess water. Fluff the bulgur to separate the grains. Now it's ready to use.

Carob

A powder made from the brown fruit or pod of the carob or locust tree (often called St. John's bread), found along the shores of the Mediterranean. It resembles unsweetened cocoa powder both in texture and taste and can act as a substitute for those who are allergic to chocolate. It is used to flavor puddings and candies and to make carob syrup. Both carob powder and carob syrup are available in most health food stores.

Chickpeas (garbanzo beans)

Round, marble-like beans used for making *Hummus Bi Tahini*, page 40, or *Falafel*, page 107.

Chickpeas are available in most supermarkets in both their canned and dried form. The canned chickpeas need only be drained to be ready to use. To prepare dried chickpeas, put ¾ cup of dried chickpeas in a medium bowl, cover with water to the top of the bowl, and soak overnight. Drain, put in a saucepan, and cover with fresh water. Cover and bring to a boil, then reduce the heat and cook until soft, about 1 hour. Drain and cool. This makes about 2 cups cooked chickpeas.

Cilantro

The Spanish name given to the leaves of the coriander plant, a member of the parsley family. To confuse matters, cilantro is also called Chinese parsley and the leaves do resemble regular parsley in shape although not in taste. They have a pungent, penetrating aroma and taste and are used in many Middle Eastern, Mediterranean, and Oriental dishes. Cilantro is available in Oriental or Latin groceries and the specialty produce section of most supermarkets.

Clarified Butter

Butter which is melted and skimmed of all its sediment, impurities, and dairy solids. In the case of melted salted butter, the salt is also removed. The remaining liquid is a clear transparent yellow. When cooled, clarified butter solidifies and becomes opaque. Because it develops its own built-in preservative as it is heated, clarified butter does not need to be refrigerated, however, for long-term storage it is best kept under refrigeration. See page 56 for information on how to clarify butter.

Coriander

An herbaceous plant of the parsley family which bears seed-like fruit with a pleasing aromatic taste. Morocco supplies most of the world's crop. The tiny seeds must be thoroughly dried before their characteristic flavor and fragrance develops. When crushed or ground their aroma and flavor is like a combination of anise, cumin, and orange peel. Coriander is available in the spice section of supermarkets as both ground and whole seeds. It is used to season many savory dishes.

The leaves of fresh coriander are called cilantro (see above).

Cumin

A spice gathered from a low-growing plant native to the Mediterranean, cumin is probably most familiar as the major ingredient in curry and chili powders. It is also used as a pungent seasoning in dips, salad and sandwich mixtures, dressings, sauces, and rice dishes. It is available in the spice section of supermarkets both as a dusty gold powder and as whole seeds.

Curry Powder

A blend of ground spices including turmeric, fenugreek, cumin, coriander, and cayenne that is commonly used in Indian cuisine. Some blends such as Madras curry powder are more assertive and pungent than others. Madras curry powder is available in the imported food and/or gourmet sections of most supermarkets.

Fava Beans

A member of the legume family, fava beans have broad pods and large flat seeds. They are used in making Egyptian Bean Croquettes, page 107, or combined with chickpeas to make *Falafel,* page 107. Kidney or similar beans make excellent substitutes. Fava beans are available in health food stores and Middle Eastern groceries.

Feta Cheese

A crumbly white cheese usually made of sheep's milk and ripened in a brine solution. There are mild, medium, and sharp feta cheeses, depending on how long they have been aged prior to being immersed in the brine. Feta is generally sold directly from the brine solution, which may be made from milk and salt or water and salt. Six ounces of feta equals 1 lightly packed cup. Feta is available in cheese shops, Greek groceries, and most supermarkets.

Figs

There are some 800 varieties of figs, varying in shape and color. The fig has been cultivated since the earliest civilization and was regarded as a symbol of peace and plenty by the early Hebrews. Two of the most common varieties are the Calimyrna which is a combination of the California and Smyrna varieties and the Black Mission fig. The Calimyrna fig is a large, squat-shaped white fig with a smooth, yellowish-green skin. The Black Mission fig is a dark purple, almost black variety with small seeds. Both are available fresh, usually from June through October, in fruit markets and most supermarkets. Dried figs are available in supermarkets and health food stores.

Garbanzo Beans

See Chickpeas.

Harissa

A pungent paste made from hot chiles and used as a condiment, dipping sauce, or as a dressing for pita sandwiches. See page 108 for the recipe. Similar hot sauces are available in Middle Eastern groceries.

Jiban

A firm, textured, fresh white cheese made from whole milk and blended with yogurt and fresh lemon juice to form a curd. The curd is removed from the whey, pressed into patties, salted, and stored in some of the reserved whey, or seasoned, tied into a cheesecloth bag, and marinated in olive oil. See page 36 for the recipe. Jiban is also available in Middle Eastern groceries.

Kasseri

A firm, white or cream-colored cheese generally made of sheep's or goat's milk. It is eaten plain, used in salads, or fried in cubes. Although Kasseri is of Greek origin, it is also found in the Balkan countries where it is called by similar names. It is usually imported but is also made domestically. It is available in cheese shops and Middle Eastern groceries.

Labani (yogurt cheese)

A soft cheese similar in texture to softened cream cheese but with a more tangy flavor. It is made from draining the water or whey from yogurt and is used as a spread or as an ingredient in appetizers and main dishes. See page 33 for the recipe. Labani is available in Middle Eastern groceries and many cheese shops.

Nopalitos

The leaves of the prickly pear cactus plant family (genus Opuntia), with the prickles removed. Nopalitos are parboiled, cooled, sliced or shredded, and used as a vegetable or as an ingredient in salads and appetizers. They are also available in cans or jars at Spanish or Mexican groceries, or by mail order from Casa Moneo, 210 West 14th Street, New York, NY 10014 (212) 929-1644.

Olive oil

A mono-unsaturated oil made from the fruit of the olive tree. A good extra virgin olive oil (made from the first pressing) is traditionally used in Middle Eastern salad and dip recipes because it imparts a characteristically savory flavor and aroma. Use olive oil also for frying or sautéeing when it is specifically recommended as it will impart a classic flavor to the finished dish. For all other frying and sautéeing, use a pure vegetable oil.

Olives

Of the many varieties of black olives available, my favorites are Alphonse and Calamara. Alfonse olives are very large, purplish-black Greek olives with with a soft texture and assertive flavor. Calamata olives are small, oval-shaped, almost-black Greek olives with a firm texture and assertive flavor. Both are available in Middle Eastern groceries, gourmet food shops, and the imported food section of most supermarkets. See page 82 for information on how to marinate olives.

Orange-blossom water

A distilled liquid made from orange blossoms and used to flavor beverages, syrups, pastries, and desserts. Rose water, made from rose petals, is a similar liquid and an excellent alternative. Both orange-blossom water and rose water are available in Middle Eastern groceries.

Pine nuts (pignolis)

Small white or cream-colored nuts from the inside of the hard outer casing of the pine cone. They are used for main dishes, stuffings, and salads, or, when toasted, as a garnish or topping. They are available in gourmet food shops and the spice section of supermarkets. To toast pine nuts on top of the range, spread them in a well-seasoned cast-iron skillet or skillet with non-stick surface. Cook over medium heat, shaking frequently, until the pine nuts turn golden-brown and smell fragrant, about 5 to 8 minutes. To toast pine nuts in the oven, preheat the oven to 350°F. Spread the pine nuts on a shallow baking tray and bake, shaking frequently, until golden-brown and fragrant, about 8 to 10 minutes.

Rose Water

See Orange-Blossom Water.

Salonika Peppers

Small, pungent, elongated, yellowish-green peppers of the capsicum family, Salonika peppers vary from mild to very hot. Commonly called Greek salad peppers, they are picked and imported in bulk from Greece and packed by various distributors in the United States. Similar varieties from other countries, such as the Italian counterpart pepperoncini, make excellent substitutes. Salonika peppers are available in Middle Eastern groceries, gourmet food shops, and the imported food section of most supermarkets.

Sesame seeds (benne)

Small cream-colored seeds from a tropical and sub-tropical herbaceous plant, sesame seeds are used to sprinkle on top of breads, pastries, and candies, as well as being the basis of sesame oil, Tahini (sesame seed paste), page 41, and the confection, halvah. They are available in supermarkets, health food stores, and Middle Eastern groceries. Sesame seeds contain a great deal of oil. To prevent them from going rancid, store them in an airtight container in the refrigerator. Use within 3 months and always take a trial sniff before including them in a recipe. If they have the aroma or flavor of old used oil, do not use them. To toast sesame seeds on top of the range, spread them in a well-seasoned cast-iron skillet or skillet with a non-stick surface. Cook over medium heat, shaking frequently, until fragrant and light golden, about 5 minutes. To toast sesame seeds in the oven, preheat the oven to 350°F. Spread the sesame seeds on a shallow baking tray and bake, shaking frequently, until fragrant and light golden, about 8 minutes.

String Cheese

An unusual Middle Eastern fresh cheese much like homemade mozzarella in consistency and texture. It is braided and seasoned with the crushed kernel or pit of the black cherry (*mahleb*) and whole black caraway seeds (*habet il baraky*). As you untwist it, pull it into strings and use as an appetizer cheese with pita. String cheese is available in Middle Eastern groceries and most cheese shops.

Sumac

A tart seasoning made from the dried ground seeds of a non-poisonous variety of the cashew plant. (The sumac herb is imported; it is not the same species of sumac that Americans know as poison su- mac.) Sumac is used as a primary ingredient in *zahter* (see below), a blend of herbs often used as a topping for pita. It is available in Middle Eastern groceries.

Tahini (sesame seed paste)

An oily paste made from ground sesame seeds and used to make sauces, dips, and dressings. Tahini is so common throughout the Mediterranean that no home is without it. See page 41 for the recipe. Tahini is also available ready-made in health food stores, Middle Eastern groceries, and the imported food section of most supermarkets.

Wheat Germ

The rich embryo of the wheat grain which is the fat-containing portion of the wheat kernel. It has a high concentration of nutrients—vitamins B and E and minerals. It is available in health food stores as toasted Regular wheat-germ, which is recommended for use in Wheat-Germ Honey Pita, page 24, and as Honey Crunch wheat-germ. Add it to bread dough and casseroles and sprinkle it over cereal, soups, and desserts.

White Cheese

See *Jiban*.

Yogurt Cheese

See *Labani*.

Zahter

A blend of marjoram, thyme, toasted sesame seeds, and the tart, dried ground seeds of the sumac plant. It is used for seasoning breads and salads. *Zahter* is available in Middle Eastern groceries. You can make an acceptable substitute by mixing 1 teaspoon each of toasted sesame seeds, powdered marjoram, powdered thyme, freshly grated lemon rind, and a dash of salt. Store with other spices in a cool, dry place.

INDEX